WIGTON

(On back)

(Crossbones and skull)

ADHERENCE
TO   SCOTLANDS   RE
FORMATION COVE
NANTS NATIONAL
AND SOLEM LEAGUE
AGED   63   1685

(3) A small upright stone :

(On top)

MEMENTO MORI

(On front)

N

HERE LYSE WILLIAM JOHNSTO
JOHN MILROY GEORGE WALKER
WHO   WAS   WITHOUT   SENTE
NCE OF LAW HANGED BY MA
JOR WINRAM FOR THEIR ADHER
ANCE   TO   SCOTLANDS   REFOR
MATION   COVENANTS   NATIO
NAL   AND   SOLAM   LEAGWE
1685.

SCOTLAND DURING THE PLANTATION OF ULSTER

The People of Dumfries and Galloway
1600–1699

by
David Dobson

CLEARFIELD

Printed for
Clearfield Company by
Genealogical Publishing Co.
Baltimore, Maryland
2008

ISBN-13: 978-0-8063-5387-6
ISBN-10: 0-8063-5387-2

Made in the United States of America

INTRODUCTION

Scotland during the seventeenth century was a nation in transition. The Union of the Crowns of Scotland and England in 1603 resulted in significant changes in the relationships between the two countries, which led to a degree of cooperation between them, such as the elimination of cross-border rustling or reiving which had existed for centuries, the expansion of trade, and a degree of collaboration in colonial ventures. This latter feature was particularly important for Ulster during the seventeenth century. For centuries English monarchs had tried, with limited success, to subjugate Ireland and under the later Tudors had made serious attempts to settle or "plant" Ireland with English colonists. The Flight of the Earls in 1607 resulted in much of Ulster falling into the hands of the new King of England, James I, who developed a plan to settle Ulster with Protestants. The earlier Plantations had been formed by immigrants from England; but this time King James, as King James VI of Scotland, invited Scots to participate. The Plantation of Ulster was inhabited by both English and Scottish settlers. "Undertakers," who were granted vast estates, were required to develop these lands and bring in settlers from Scotland and England. As far as the Scots Undertakers were concerned, they generally recruited settlers from among their tenants in Scotland. As many of these Undertakers came from south west Scotland, many of the Scots who settled in Ulster came from there also.

While economic opportunity was the major factor attracting the Scots to Ulster in the seventeenth century, other factors were influential, such as the persecution of the Covenanters which drove many from south west Scotland into emigration or exile in later centuries. It should also be noted that one of the earliest attempts by the Scots to settle in North America was organised from Kirkcudbright by Sir Robert Gordon of Lochinvar in 1622 bound for Cape Breton. The opportunities and the close proximity of Ireland, however, discouraged transatlantic emigration in favour of Ulster.

This book is designed as an aid to family historians researching their origins in the counties of Dumfries-shire, Kirkcudbright-shire, and Wigtown-shire, now known as Dumfries and Galloway. Scottish genealogical research is primarily based on the Old Parish Registers of the Church of Scotland; however, for Dumfries and Galloway only three of the eighty-six such registers date from before 1685. This source book, therefore, to some extent overcomes the lack of accessible records. It is based, overwhelmingly, on primary sources in the National Archives of Scotland in Edinburgh and is fully referenced. A wide range of sources have been used in the compilation of this book including the Court of Session, the Commissary Courts of Dumfries and Edinburgh, the High Court of the Admiralty, Kirk Session Records, burgh records, Registers of Deeds, Retours, Customs records, and monumental inscriptions. The book does not claim to be a comprehensive listing but rather a selection taken from various sources to illustrate what is available to researchers. The major families in this region of Scotland included Irving, Kennedy, Gordon, Maxwell, McKie, McLellan, McDowall, and Johnston, many of whom are featured in this book.

David Dobson
St Andrews, Scotland, 2008

REFERENCES

CalSPIre   Calendar of State Papers,
        Ireland
CLC   =   Calendar of the Laing
        Charters, 854-1837
DAC   =   Dumfries Archives Centre
DSA   =   Delaware State Archives
F=   Fasti Ecclesiae Scoticanae
FI   =   Fasti of the Irish Presbyterian
        Church
LCC   =   Lochmaben Court and
        Council Book, 1612-1721,
                [Edinburgh, 2001]
NAS   =   National Archives of Scotland
NEHGS   New England Historic
        Genealogical Society
PCC   =   Prerogative Court of
        Canterbury
PHS   =   Presbyterian Historical
        Society
RBM   =   R. B. Miller, research papers
RGS   =   Register of the Great Seal of
        Scotland
RPCS   =   Register of the Privy Council
        of Scotland
SCS   =   Scottish Charitable Society

FLAG OF THE COVENANTERS.

SCOTLAND DURING THE PLANTATION OF ULSTER:

THE PEOPLE OF DUMFRIES AND GALLOWAY, 1600–1699

A'BARRON, MICHAEL, in Kilhill, parish of Inch, testament, 1593, Commissary of Edinburgh. [NAS]

ACHESON, ADAM, in Auchenslark, parish of Dryfesdale, 1620. [NAS.CS7/335/294]

ACHESON, CHRISTIAN, in the parish of Dryfesdale, 1620. [NAS.CS7/335/294]

ACHESON, JAMES, in Bishopcleuch, parish of Dryfesdale, 1620. [NAS.CS7/335/294]

ACHESON, JOHN, in Corryfin, parish of Moffat, 1620. [NAS.CS7/335/265]

ACHESON, JOHN, in the parish of Moffat, 1620. [NAS.CS7/335/265]

ACHESON, ROBERT, in Polmuthie, parish of Moffat, 1620. [NAS.CS7/335/265]

ACHESON, THOMAS, in the parish of Moffat, 1620. [NAS.CS7/335/265]

ACHESON, WILLIAM, in Torwood, parish of Dryfesdale, 1620. [NAS.CS7/335/294]

ADAIR, PATRICK, born 1675, son of William Adair in Corgie, Galloway, educated at the Universities of Edinburgh and Glasgow, graduated MA from Glasgow University in 1694, minister of Carrickfergus from 1702, died 12 June 1717. [FI.89]

ADAIR, WILLIAM, heir to his father Ninian Adair of Kinhilt, 1608. [NAS.Retours. Wigtown#33]

ADAMSON, AGNES, in Lawstoun, parish of Lochrutton, 1620. [NAS.CS7/ 335]

ADAMSON, JAMES, and his spouse Marie Cavart, in Little Dalton, testament, 1683, Commissary of Dumfries. [NAS]

ADAMSON, JOHN, in Sherington, parish of Caerlaverock, 1619. [NAS.CS7/ 335/109]

ADAMSON, JOHN, in Rigside, parish of Dumfries, testament, 1638, Commissary of Dumfries. [NAS]

ADAMSON, JOHN, son of the late John Adamson, a merchant burgess of Dumfries, testament, 1657, Commissary of Dumfries. [NAS]

ADAMSON, MARION, in Carswada, parish of Lochrutton, 1620. [NAS.CS7/ 335/311]

ADAMSON, THOMAS, in the Netherfield of the Mains of Caerlaverock, testament, 1659, Commissary of Dumfries. [NAS]

ADARE, ROBERT, from Galloway, probate 1692 Barbados.

A'DRYNAN, HERBERT, in Fynnarts, Glenape, parish of Kirkcudbright, spouse Mallie MacIlwaine, testament, 1591, Commissary of Edinburgh. [NAS]

AFFLECK, JOHN, in Deanstoun, parish of Lochrutton, 1620. [NAS.CS7.335.311]

AGNEW, ANDREW, heir to his father Alexander Agnew of Croach, 1680. [NAS.Retours.Wigtown#160]

AGNEW, Sir PATRICK, of Lochnaw, leased lands near Larne, 1636. [NAS.GD154.505]

A'HANNA, JOHN, in Carsuada, parish of Lochrutton, 1620. [NAS.CS7.335.311]

AIKINE, JOHN, died in 1662. [Colvend gravestone]

AITCHESON, ANDREW, in Blacketlies, testament, 1684, Commissary of Dumfries. [NAS]

AITCHISON, EDWARD, in Clerkhill, testament, 1679, Commissary of Dumfries. [NAS]

AITCHISON, HERBERT, in Polmadie, parish of Moffat, testament, 1638, Commissary of Dumfries. [NAS]

AITCHISON, JOHN, in Bosbeg, testament, 1661, Commissary of Dumfries. [NAS]

AITCHESON, WILLIAM, in Commertrees, testament, 1681, Commissary of Dumfries. [NAS]

AITKEN, ANDREW, burgess of Dumfries, testament, 1643, Commissary of Dumfries. [NAS]

AITKEN, JAMES, in Auchenlosh, testament, 1657, Commissary of Dumfries. [NAS]

AITKEN, JOHN, in Dincow, testament, 1656, Commissary of Dumfries. [NAS]

AITKEN, JOHN, in Breakingside, testament, 1657, Commissary of Dumfries. [NAS]

AITKEN, JOHN, in Barscreach, testament, 1659, Commissary of Dumfries. [NAS]

AITKEN, JOHN, in Meikle Cloak, testament, 1673, Commissary of Dumfries. [NAS]

AITKEN, JOHN, a merchant burgess of Dumfries, testament, 1679, Commissary of Dumfries. [NAS]

AITKEN, JOHN, in Jackligg of Southwick, testament, 1683, Commissary of Dumfries. [NAS]

AITKEN, ROGER, in Woodhouse, parish of Colvend, testament, 1642, Commissary of Dumfries. [NAS]

AITKEN, ROGER, in Ryes, parish of Southwick, testament, 1685/1686, Commissary of Dumfries. [NAS]

AITKEN, ROGER, the younger of Auchinhay, testament, 1686, Commissary of Dumfries. [NAS]

ALEXANDER, JOHN, in Rigside of Redkirk, testament, 1659, Commissary of Dumfries. [NAS]

ALEXANDER, JOHN, master of the Adventure of Dumfries, sailing to Danzig and France, 1680s. [NAS.E72.6.7/8/9/10]

ALEXANDER, JOHN, minister at Hoddam, testament, 1687, Commissary of Dumfries. [NAS]

ALEXANDER, ROBERT, in Guffockland, parish of Kirkconnell, testament, 1638, Commissary of Dumfries. [NAS]

ALFIE, ANDREW, in Barquhenny, parish of Kirkinner, spouse Margaret Carsane, testament, 1592, Commissary of Edinburgh. [NAS]

ALISE, EDWARD, testament, 1657, Commissary of Dumfries. [NAS]

ALISON, BESSIE, in Little Dalton, testament, 1659, Commissary of Dumfries. [NAS]

ALISON, JOHN, in Little Dalton. testament, 1657, Commissary of Dumfries. [NAS]

ALISON, JOHN, of Glencorse, testament, 1686, Commissary of Dumfries. [NAS]

ALISON, WILLIAM, minister at Dornock, testament, 1685, Commissary of Dumfries. [NAS]

ALLAN, FERGUS, in Hills, parish of Lochrutton, 1620. [NAS.CS7/335]

ALLAN, JOHN, in Lawstoun, parish of Lochrutton, 1620. [NAS.CS7.335.311]

ALLAN, PATRICK, with Janet Vetch and their son James Allan, arrived in Dumfries by 1696 from Ireland. [NAS.CH2.537.15.1/161-165]

ALLAN, QUINTIN, in Stockford, parish of Moffat, 1620. [NAS.CS7/335/265]

ALLAN, RICHARD, in Bowrig, parish of Lochrutton, 1620. [NAS.CS7/335]

ALLAN, RICHIE, in Carsuada, parish of Lochrutton, 1620. [NAS.CS7.335.311]

ALLAN, ROBERT, in Lawstoun, parish of Lochrutton, 1620. [NAS.CS7/335]

ALLAN, PATRICK, in Hills, parish of Lochrutton, 1620. [NAS.CS7/335]

ALLAN, THOMAS, in Langrigsland, parish of Caerlaverock, 1619. [NAS.CS7/335/109]

ALLAN, THOMAS, minister at Wauchop, testament, 1685, Commissary of Dumfries. [NAS]

A'MULLIGAN, ABRAHAM, a merchant in Holm of Dalquharn in the parish of Dalry, testament, 1603, Commissary of Edinburgh. [NAS]

ANDERSON, ANDREW, in Dalskairth, testament, 1680, Commissary of Dumfries. [NAS]

ANDERSON, ARCHIBALD, in Outbyre, testament, 1687, Commissary of Dumfries. [NAS]

ANDERSON, HOMER, Deacon of the Fleshers of Dumfries, 1661. [DAC]

ANDERSON, HUGH, in Carruchen, testament, 1685, Commissary of Dumfries. [NAS]

ANDERSON, JAMES, in Drumganes, testament, 1643, Commissary of Dumfries. [NAS]

ANDERSON, JAMES, in Dalbeattie, testament, 1657, Commissary of Dumfries. [NAS]

ANDERSON, JANET, a widow, arrived in Dumfries during 1691 from Ireland. [NAS.CH2.537.15.1/73-94]

ANDERSON, JOHN, in the parish of Caerlaverock, 1619. [NAS.CS7/335/109]

ANDERSON, JOHN, in Burncleugh, testament, 1628, Commissary of Dumfries. [NAS]

ANDERSON, JOHN, in Craigcroft, testament, 1678, Commissary of Dumfries. [NAS]

ANDERSON, JOHN, in Terregles, testament, 1683, Commissary of Dumfries. [NAS]

ANDERSON, JOHN, in Shalloch, testament, 1686, Commissary of Dumfries. [NAS]

ANDERSON, MICHAEL, of Kilcrest, testament, 1683, Commissary of Dumfries. [NAS]

ANDERSON, PATRICK, in Filend, testament, 1624, Commissary of Dumfries. [NAS]

ANDERSON, ROBERT, a merchant in Dumfries, 1621. [NAS.E71.10.5]

ANDERSON, ROBERT, in Mosscroft, testament, 1630, Commissary of Dumfries. [NAS]

ANDERSON, ROBERT, in Dyke, spouse Agnes Black, testament, 1642, Commissary of Edinburgh. [NAS]

ANDERSON, ROBERT, the elder, in Preston, testament, 1658, Commissary of Dumfries. [NAS]

ANDERSON, RODGER, a burgess of Dumfries, testament, 1673, Commissary of Dumfries. [NAS]

ANDERSON, WILLIAM, the elder, in Shalloch, testament, 1678, Commissary of Dumfries. [NAS]

ARCHIBALD, CHARLES, minister at Kirkbean, testament, 1658, 1661, Commissary of Dumfries. [NAS]

ARCHIBALDSON, CUTHBERT, a merchant burgess of Dumfries, testament, 1591, Commissary of Edinburgh. [NAS]

ARMSTRONG, ADAM, in Tarrona, testament, 1679, Commissary of Dumfries. [NAS]

ARMSTRONG, ADAM, in Alvierig, testament, 1682, Commissary of Dumfries. [NAS]

ARMSTRONG, ANDREW, in Rowanburn, testament, 1673, Commissary of Dumfries. [NAS]

ARMSTRONG, ARCHIBALD, in Corrie, testament, 1685, Commissary of Dumfries. [NAS]

ARMSTRONG, GEORGE, in Blackbeckhead, testament, 1626, Commissary of Dumfries. [NAS]

ARMSTRONG, GEORGE, a merchant in Langholm, testament, 1643, Commissary of Dumfries. [NAS]

ARMSTRONG, GEORGE, of Kinmont, a refugee in Ireland, 1679. [RPCS.VI.159]

ARMSTRONG, JOHN, of Sorbie, testament, 1687, Commissary of Dumfries. [NAS]

ARMSTRONG, JOHN, in Neishill, testament, 1692, Commissary of Dumfries. [NAS]

ARMSTRONG, LANCE, a thief, brother of Andrew Armstrong of Kirkton, was banished to Ireland on 10 June 1620. [RPCS.XII.288]

ARMSTRONG, MARGARET, in Mosspebbles, testament, 1657, Commissary of Dumfries. [NAS]

ARMSTRONG, ROBERT, in Howhouse, testament, 1682, Commissary of Dumfries. [NAS]

ARMSTRONG, THOMAS, a thief, brother of Andrew Armstrong of Kirkton, was banished to Ireland on 10 June 1620. [RPCS.XII.288]; later apprehended in Ireland and returned to Scotland where he was imprisoned in Dumfries Tolbooth in 1632. [RPCS.IV.496]

ARMSTRONG, THOMAS, in Bethhill, testament, 1656, Commissary of Dumfries. [NAS]

ARMSTRONG, THOMAS, in Bograe, testament, 1679, Commissary of Dumfries. [NAS]

ARMSTRONG, THOMAS, in Broomknow, testament, 1682, Commissary of Dumfries. [NAS]

ARMSTRONG, THOMAS, of Nethercraig, testament, 1688, Commissary of Dumfries. [NAS]

ARMSTRONG, WILLIAM, a merchant in Dumfries, 1621. [NAS.E71.10.5]

ARMSTRONG, WILLIAM, in Hillside, testament, 1679, Commissary of Dumfries. [NAS]

ARMSTRONG, WILLIAM, son of Michael Armstrong, in Outerwoodhead, testament, 1679, Commissary of Dumfries. [NAS]

ARMSTRONG, WILLIAM, in Kilburnie, spouse Jean Armstrong, testament, 1686, Commissary of Dumfries. [NAS]

ARNOTT, DAVID, Customs controller of Kirkcudbright, 1614-1615. [NAS.E74.2.7]

ARTHUR, HARBERT, a cooper burgess of Dumfries, testament, 1625, Commissary of Dumfries. [NAS]

ASHINNAN, GEORGE, in Thifmains, parish of Balmaghie, 1619. [NAS.CS7/335/63]

ASHENAN, WILLIAM, in Beoch, spouse Janet Reid, testament 1596, testament, 1596, Commissary of Edinburgh. [NAS]

A'SLOAN, JOHN, in Ingliston, parish of Glencairn, spouse Janet Howieson, testament, 1595, Commissary of Edinburgh. [NAS]

A'SLOWAN, GEORGE, in Camdudzeil, testament, 1592, Commissary of Edinburgh. [NAS]

BAILLIE, JOHN, in Skeich, parish of Penninghame, testament, 1599, Commissary of Edinburgh. [NAS]

BAILLIE, JOHN, in Little Dunragat, parish of Glenluce, testament, 1600, Commissary of Edinburgh. [NAS]

BAILLIE, ROBERT, a merchant burgess of Dumfries, testament, 1685, Commissary of Dumfries. [NAS]

BAIRDINE, THOMAS, testament, 1657, Commissary of Dumfries. [NAS]

BAITTIE, JOHN, in the parish of Caerlaverock, 1619. [NAS.CS7/335/109]

BARBOUR, JANET, in Laggan, testament, 1659, Commissary of Dumfries. [NAS]

BARBOUR, JOHN, in Waterhead, testament, 1629, Commissary of Dumfries. [NAS]

BARBOUR, WILLIAM, in Ingliston, parish of Durisdeer, testament, 1638, Commissary of Dumfries. [NAS]

BARNECLEUTH, MUNGO, in the parish of Kirkpatrick-Irongray, testament, 1626, Commissary of Dumfries. [NAS]

BARRICK, WILLIAM, in Lochrutton, testament, 1591, Commissary of Edinburgh. [NAS]

BARTON, ROBERT, a notary, testament, 1676, Commissary of Dumfries. [NAS]

BARTON, ROBERT, a drover in Mouswald, deed, 1699. [NAS.RD2.82.911]

BARTON, THOMAS, at Nethermilne, parish of Moffat, 1620. [NAS.CS7/335/265]

BARTON, THOMAS, in Cottmipen, testament, 1659, Commissary of Dumfries. [NAS]

BATTIE, JOHN, a merchant in Dumfries, 1621. [NAS.E71.10.5]

BAXTER, DAVID, a merchant in Dumfries, 1622. [NAS.E71.10.5]

BEATTIE, ARTHUR, in Woodend, testament, 1682, Commissary of Dumfries. [NAS]

BEATTIE, GEORGE, in Coopwood, parish of Dryfesdale, 1620. [NAS.CS7/335/294]

BEATTIE, GEORGE, in Coopwood, parish of Dryfesdale, 1620. [NAS.CS7/335/294]

BEATTIE, DAVID, in the parish of Moffat, 1620. [NAS.CS7/335/265]

BEATTIE, DICK, in Coopwood, parish of Dryfesdale, 1620. [NAS.CS7/335/294]

BEATTIE, HEW, in the parish of Westerkirk, testament, 1642, Commissary of Dumfries. [NAS]

BEATTIE, HUGH, miller at Hookmilne, testament, 1687, Commissary of Dumfries. [NAS]

BEATTIE, JAMES, in Burnfoot, testament, 1682, Commissary of Dumfries. [NAS]

BEATTIE, JEAN, in Woodhouselies, testament, 1676, Commissary of Dumfries. [NAS]

BEATTIE, JOHN, a burgess of Dumfries, testament, 1598, Commissary of Edinburgh. [NAS]

BEATTIE, JOHN, of Burn, parish of Westerkirk, testament, 1659, Commissary of Dumfries. [NAS]

BEATTIE, JOHN, in Torrcune, testament, 1687, Commissary of Dumfries. [NAS]

BEATTIE, JOHN, in Clerkhill, parish of Westerkirk, testament, 1693, Commissary of Dumfries. [NAS]

BEATTIE, JOHN, in Broadlee, spouse Blanche Carlisle, testament, 1676, Commissary of Dumfries. [NAS]

BEATTIE, MICHAEL, in Hillhead, parish of Dryfesdale, 1620. [NAS.CS7/335/294]

BEATTIE, THOMAS, in Datonhook, parish of Dryfesdale, 1620. [NAS.CS7/335/294]

BEATTIE, THOMAS, a merchant burgess of Dumfries, testament, 1638, Commissary of Dumfries. [NAS]

BEATTIE, THOMAS, in Bengall, testament, 1657, Commissary of Dumfries. [NAS]

BEATTIE, THOMAS, in Kirslitt, testament, 1673, Commissary of Dumfries. [NAS]

BEATTIE, WALTER, in Dinfedlin, testament, 1656, Commissary of Dumfries. [NAS]

BEATTIE, WALTER, in Dongland, testament, 1681, Commissary of Dumfries. [NAS]

BEATTIE, WILLIAM, in Lockerbie, parish of Dryfesdale, 1620. [NAS.CS7/335/294]

BEATTIE, WILLIAM, in Burnfoot, testament, 1631, Commissary of Dumfries. [NAS]

BEATTIE, WILLIAM, spouse Janet Armstrong, testament, 1640, Commissary of Dumfries. [NAS]

BEATTIE, WILLIAM, son of the late John Beattie, in Burn, parish of Westerkirk, testament, 1642, Commissary of Dumfries. [NAS]

BEATTIE, WILLIAM, in Watcarrick, testament, 1656, Commissary of Dumfries. [NAS]

BEATTIE, WILLIAM, in Milton, testament, 1682, Commissary of Dumfries. [NAS]

BEATTIE, WILLIAM, in Skipmyre, testament, 1689, Commissary of Dumfries. [NAS]

BECK, JOHN, a cordiner at the Bridgend of Dumfries, testament, 1683, Commissary of Dumfries. [NAS]

BECK, JOHN, in Dalswinton, testament, 1684, Commissary of Dumfries. [NAS]

BELL, ADAM, in Newton of Kirkchrist, testament, 1592, Commissary of Edinburgh. [NAS]

BELL, ADAM, in Nether Mossop, parish of Moffat, 1620. [NAS.CS7/335/ 265]

BELL, ALEXANDER, in Luce, testament, 1638, Commissary of Dumfries. [NAS]

BELL, ALEXANDER, and his spouse Nicola Murray, in Drumstenchell, testament, 1686, Commissary of Dumfries. [NAS]

BELL, DAVID, in Kirkconnell, testament, 1658, Commissary of Dumfries. [NAS]

BELL, DAVID, in Lie, testament, 1686, Commissary of Dumfries. [NAS]

BELL, GEORGE, in the parish of Moffat, 1620. [NAS.CS7/335/265]

BELL, GEORGE, in Crofthead, parish of Dryfesdale, 1620. [NAS.CS7/335/ 294]

BELL, HARBERT, in Drysdalegait, parish of Dryfesdale, 1620. [NAS.CS7/ 335/294]

BELL, JAMES, in Lockerbie, parish of Dryfesdale, 1620. [NAS.CS7/335/ 294]

BELL, JAMES, in Moss-side, spouse Helen Beattie, testament, 1676, Commissary of Dumfries. [NAS]

BELL, JOHN, in Whiteyards, parish of Lochrutton, 1620. [NAS.CS7.335.311]

BELL, JOHN, in Lockerbie, parish of Dryfesdale, 1620. [NAS.CS7/335/294]

BELL, JOHN, in Corhead, parish of Moffat, 1620. [NAS.CS7/335/265]

BELL, JOHN, in the parish of Moffat, 1620. [NAS.CS7/335/265]

BELL, JOHN, in Torwood, parish of Dryfesdale, 1620. [NAS.CS7/335/294]

BELL, JOHN, in Archland, spouse Margaret Halliday born 1555, died 27 January 1631. [Anwoth gravestone]

BELL, JOHN, of Whitesyde, a Covenanter killed in the parish of Tongland by government troops in 1685. [Anwoth gravestone]

BELL, JOHN, in Slork, parish of Drysdale, spouse Bessie Bell, testament, 1691, Commissary of Dumfries. [NAS]

BELL, JUNKIN, in Newton, spouse Blanch Bell, testament, 1657, Commissary of Dumfries. [NAS]

BELL, MARTIN, in Datonhook, parish of Dryfesdale, 1620. [NAS.CS7/335/294]

BELL, PET, in Mantuarig, parish of Dryfesdale, 1620. [NAS.CS7/335/294]

BELL, RICHIE, in Auldwalls, parish of Dryfesdale, 1620. [NAS.CS7/335/294]

BELL, ROBERT, master of the Robert of Dumfries, 1690. [NAS.E72.6.18/20/21]

BELL, THOMAS, in Deinstoun, parish of Lochrutton, 1620. [NAS.CS7/335/311]

BELL, WALTER, in Wintropheid, spouse Agnes Armstrong, testament, 1657, Commissary of Dumfries. [NAS]

BELL, WILLIAM, in the parish of Moffat, 1620. [NAS.CS7/335/265]

BELL, WILLIAM, in Millpath, parish of Middlebie, testament, 1680, Commissary of Dumfries. [NAS]

BELL, WILLIAM, heir to his brother George Bell of Scottsbridge, 1697. [NAS.Retours, Dumfries#348]

BELLIS, DAVID, a merchant in Dumfries, trading with Flanders, 1622. [NAS.E71.10.5]

BENNOCH, JOHN, in Nether Tormolland, parish of Balmaghie, 1619. [NAS.CS7/335/63]

BICKERTON, ANDREW, in Cormehead, parish of Lochrutton, 1620. [NAS.CS7/335/311]

BICKERTON, ANDREW, the younger, in Bar, parish of Lochrutton, 1620. [NAS.CS7/335/311]

BICKERTON, FLORA, in Balfill, parish of Lochrutton, 1620. [NAS.CS7.335.311]

BICKERTON, WILLIAM, in Netherdeadside, parish of Lochrutton, 1620. [NAS.CS7/335/311]

BIGHOLM, PETER, a merchant in Glencairn, testament, 1600, Commissary of Edinburgh. [NAS]

BIRNIE, WALTER, in Stableton, testament, 1673, Commissary of Edinburgh. [NAS]

BIRRELL, GEORGE, in Tordoch, testament, 1658, Commissary of Dumfries. [NAS]

BISHOP, DAVID, late provost of Dumfries, testament, 1680, Commissary of Dumfries. [NAS]

BISHOP, JOHN, in Riddings, parish of Moffat, 1620. [NAS.CS7/335/265]

BLACK, JOHN, from the Water of Orr, Galloway, a Covenanter prisoner transported from Leith to East New Jersey in 1685. [RPCS.IXI.154/291/292]

BLACK, PATRICK, the elder, in Rig, parish of Kirkconnell, testament, 1641, Commissary of Dumfries. [NAS]

BLACK, THOMAS, in Cairuchen, testament, 1598, Commissary of Edinburgh. [NAS]

BLACK, WALTER, in Murthlet, testament, 1685, Commissary of Dumfries. [NAS]

BLACK, WILLIAM, son of the late John Black, in Sanquhar, testament, 1657, Commissary of Dumfries. [NAS]

BLACK, WILLIAM, in Lafonolone, parish of Kirkconnell, testament, 1683, Commissary of Dumfries. [NAS]

BLACK, WILLIAM, minister at Closeburn, testament, 1684, Commissary of Dumfries. [NAS]

BLACKLOCK, ADAM, in Newton, testament, 1657, Commissary of Dumfries. [NAS]

BLACKLOCK, ADAM, and his relict Margaret Graham, testament, 1657, Commissary of Dumfries. [NAS]

BLACKLOCK, ANDREW, a resident of Lochmaben, 1642. [LCC#45]

BLACKLOCK, JOHN, in Nether Mossop, parish of Moffat, 1620. [NAS.CS7/335/265]

BLACKLOCK, JOHN, in Hairhope, parish of Moffat, 1620. [NAS.CS7/335/265]

BLACKLOCK, JOHN, a merchant in Dumfries, 1621. [NAS.E71.10.5]

BLACKLOCK, JOHN, in Mylnehill, testament, 1630, Commissary of Dumfries. [NAS]

BLACKLOCK, JOHN, in Park, testament, 1680, Commissary of Dumfries. [NAS]

BLACKLOCK, JOHN, a merchant, testament, 1681, Commissary of Dumfries. [NAS]

BLACKLOCK, JOHN, in Cloynyard, testament, 1683, Commissary of Dumfries. [NAS]

BLACKLOCK, MARTIN, in Nether Mossop, parish of Moffat, 1620. [NAS.CS7/335/265]

BLACKLOCK, MATHEW, a resident of Lochmaben, 1642. [LCC#45]

BLACKLOCK, PETER, in Greenhill, parish of Moffat, 1620. [NAS.CS7/335/265]

BLACKLOCK, ROBERT, in Connellbus, parish of Sanquhar, testament, 1641, Commissary of Dumfries. [NAS]

BLACKLOCK, JOHN, treasurer of the burgh of Lochmaben, 1684. [LCC#179]

BLACKLOCK, ROBERT, in Broad Chapel, testament, 1685, Commissary of Dumfries. [NAS]

BLACKLOCK, THOMAS, in Nether Mossop, parish of Moffat, 1620. [NAS.CS7/335/265]

BLACKLOCK, THOMAS, in Glen Tennant, testament, 1657, Commissary of Dumfries. [NAS]

BLACKSTOCK, EDWARD, in Steulhill, testament, 1657, Commissary of Dumfries. [NAS]

BLACKSTOCK, JOHN, in Glenhowen, parish of Caerlaverock, 1619. [NAS.CS7/335/109]

BLACKSTOCK, JOHN, a merchant burgess of Dumfries, testament, 1641, Commissary of Dumfries. [NAS]

BLACKSTOCK, MARGARET, in Rockellskaith, testament, 1658, Commissary of Dumfries. [NAS]

BLACKSTOCK, ROBERT, in Mersehead, testament, 1683, Commissary of Dumfries. [NAS]

BLACKWOOD, THOMAS, in the parish of Moffat, 1620. [NAS.CS7/335/265]

BLAIN, MICHAEL, probably from Wigtownshire, settled in Bannach, Ireland, before 1674. [Laing Charters#2728]

BLAIR, CHARLES, (?), a quarrier in Colvend, died 1670. [Colvend gravestone]

BLAIR, JAMES, master of the Mayflower of Whithorn, 1684. [NAS.AC7/6]

BLAKE, ANDREW, in Slathat, testament, 1624, Commissary of Dumfries. [NAS]

BLAKE, HERBERT, in Garrell, testament, 1656, Commissary of Dumfries. [NAS]

BLAKE, WALTER, in Garrell, testament, 1676, Commissary of Dumfries. [NAS]

BLAKE, WILLIAM, in Crockroy, testament, 1656, Commissary of Dumfries. [NAS]

BLANE, JOHN, in Barquhaskane, parish of Glenluce, testament, 1600, Commissary of Edinburgh. [NAS]

BOISHE, ANDREW, and spouse Marion Wood, in Floshend, testament, 1681, Commissary of Dumfries. [NAS]

BORTHWICK, BESSIE, in Carrit-rig, testament, 1657, Commissary of Dumfries. [NAS]

BOWIE, JEROME, testament, 1661, Commissary of Dumfries. [NAS]

BOYD, JAMES, at the Bridgend of Dumfries, testament, 1658, Commissary of Dumfries. [NAS]

BOYD, ROBERT, arrived in Dumfries during 1690 from Ireland. [NAS.CH2.537.15.1/34]

BOYIS, ANDREW, in Dryisholme, parish of Dryfesdale, 1620. [NAS.CS7/335/294]

BRAIDEN, BESSIE, in Auldwalls, parish of Dryfesdale, 1620. [NAS.CS7/335/294]

BRAIDFOOT, JOHN, in Arrow, parish of Glasserton, testament, 1600, Commissary of Edinburgh. [NAS]

BRAINZEIR, HELEN, testament, 1657, Commissary of Dumfries. [NAS]

BRAITHNOCH, ROBERT, in Auchinhay, parish of Kirkpatrick Durham, testament, 1641, Commissary of Dumfries. [NAS]

BRAND, GEORGE, a mariner from Tweedswell in Nithsdale, who died bound for the East Indies, probate 1676, PCC

BRATTON, JOHN, in Coalimpone, testament, 1682, Commissary of Dumfries. [NAS]

BRATTON, ROBERT, in Dalsible, testament, 1689, Commissary of Dumfries. [NAS]

BREICH, CHRISTOPHER, a resident of Lochmaben, 1642. [LCC#45]

BREWHOUSE, JOHN, parish of Caerlaverock, 1619. [NAS.CS7/335/109]

BRIGGS, JOHN, in Kirkbean, testament, 1656, Commissary of Dumfries. [NAS]

BRIGGS, JOHN, son to John Briggs, in Drum, testament, 1675, Commissary of Dumfries. [NAS]

BRIGGS, JOHN, in Drum, testament, 1691, Commissary of Dumfries. [NAS]

BRIGGS, WALTER, in Nimblie, testament, 1676, Commissary of Dumfries. [NAS]

BRIGGS, WILLIAM, testament, 1658, Commissary of Dumfries. [NAS]

BRIGGS, WILLIAM, in Stonedykes, testament, 1674, Commissary of Dumfries. [NAS]

BROADFOOT, JANET, in Gaitslacht, testament, 1658, Commissary of Dumfries. [NAS]

BROATCH, JAMES, in Hietae, testament, 1628, Commissary of Dumfries. [NAS]

BROATCH, JANET, in Guilylands, testament, 1659, Commissary of Dumfries. [NAS]

BROATCH, JOHN, in Gairthend, testament, 1624, Commissary of Dumfries. [NAS]

BROATCH, JOHN, former Dean of Dumfries, testament, 1691, Commissary of Dumfries. [NAS]

BROTHERSTONES, JAMES, minister at Glencairn, testament, 1679, Commissary of Dumfries. [NAS]

BROWN, ADAM, in Studrigs, testament, 1684, Commissary of Dumfries. [NAS]

BROWN, ADAM, in Branrig, testament, 1688, Commissary of Dumfries. [NAS]

BROWN, ANDREW, in Torwood, parish of Dryfesdale, 1620. [NAS.CS7/335/294]

BROWN, ARCHIE, in Auldwalls, parish of Dryfesdale, 1620. [NAS.CS7/335/294]

BROWN, CUTHBERT, in Penlego, testament, 1628, Commissary of Dumfries. [NAS]

BROWN, CUTHBERT, in Craigend, testament, 1680, Commissary of Dumfries. [NAS]

BROWN, EDMOND, of Troston, testament, 1690, Commissary of Dumfries. [NAS]

BROWN, GAVIN, of Bishopton, testaments, 1684, 1694, Commissary of Dumfries. [NAS]

BROWN, GEORGE, from Annandale, a vagabond and robber ordered to be transported to the American Plantations, 1671. [RPCS.III.428]

BROWN, GEORGE, in Moss-side, parish of Dumfries, testament, 1683, Commissary of Dumfries. [NAS]

BROWN, HELEN, in Bourlands, parish of Caerlaverock, 1619. [NAS.CS7/335/109]

BROWN, JAMES, minister at Kirkpatrick-Irongray, testaments, 1641, 1643, Commissary of Dumfries. [NAS]

BROWN, JOHN, in the parish of Caerlaverock, 1619. [NAS.CS7/335/109]

BROWN, JOHN, at Bridgend of Dumfries, 1621. [RPCS.XII.586]

BROWN, JOHN, in Durisdeer, testament, 1624, Commissary of Dumfries. [NAS]

BROWN, JOHN, in Dalswinton, testament, 1627, Commissary of Dumfries. [NAS]

BROWN, JOHN, burgess of Sanquhar, testament, 1629, Commissary of Dumfries. [NAS]

BROWN, JOHN, in Marbroy, spouse Janet Caird, testament, 1642, Commissary of Dumfries. [NAS]

BROWN, JOHN, in Torrerie, testament, 1657, Commissary of Dumfries. [NAS]

BROWN, JOHN, in Laggan, testament, 1658, Commissary of Dumfries.

BROWN, JOHN, from Annandale, a vagabond and robber ordered to be transported to the American Plantations, 1671. [RPCS.III.428]

BROWN, JOHN, in Gateside, testament, 1674, Commissary of Dumfries.

BROWN, JOHN, and his son Robert, in Trailtroue, testament, 1676, Commissary of Dumfries. [NAS]

BROWN, JOHN, a tailor in Kirkcudbright, transported to the American Plantations in 1684. [RPCS.X.258]

BROWN, JOHN, minister at Westerkirk, testament, 1688, Commissary of Dumfries. [NAS]

BROWN, MATTHEW, in Huttonhill, parish of Dryfesdale, 1620. [NAS.CS7/335/294]

BROWN, PATRICK, a merchant in Dumfries, 1622. [NAS.E71.10.5]

BROWN, PATRICK, from Annandale, a vagabond and robber ordered to be transported to the American Plantations, 1671. [RPCS.III.428]

BROWN, RICHARD, at the Kirk of Glencairn, testament, 1656, Commissary of Dumfries. [NAS]

BROWN, ROBERT, in Meikle Cloak, testament, 1682, Commissary of Dumfries. [NAS]

BROWN, THOMAS, of Glen, testament 1626, Commissary of Dumfries.

BROWN, WILLIAM, a merchant in Dumfries, 1621. [NAS.E71.10.5]

BROWN, WILLIAM, in Dargavell, testament, 1625, Commissary of Dumfries. [NAS]

BROWN, WILLIAM, minister at Glencairn, testament, 1637, Commissary of Dumfries. [NAS]

BROWN, WILLIAM, in Maidenpape, testament, 1679, Commissary of Dumfries. [NAS]

BRYCE, JOHN, died 1709. [Anwoth gravestone]

BRYDEN, JOHN, a resident of Lochmaben, 1642. [LCC#45]

BRYDEN, JOHN, in Lammock, testament, 1676, Commissary of Dumfries. [NAS]

BRYDEN, THOMAS, in Damhead, testament, 1659, Commissary of Dumfries. [NAS]

BURGESS, EDWARD, at Old Woodneuk, Holywood, testaments, 1681, 1691, Commissary of Dumfries. [NAS]

BURGESS, JAMES, a merchant burgess of Dumfries, testament, 1639, Commissary of Dumfries. [NAS]

BURGESS, JOHN, in Wraiths, testament, 1658, Commissary of Dumfries. [NAS]

BURNE, ROBERT, in Kirkpatrick, testament, 1630, Commissary of Dumfries. [NAS]

BYRES, CATHERINE, in Lochmaben, testament, 1629, Commissary of Dumfries. [NAS]

BYRES, JAMES, a weaver and councillor of Lochmaben, 1684. [LCC#179]

BYRES, JAMES, a tailor and councillor of Lochmaben, 1684. [LCC#179]

BYRES, JOHN, a councillor of Lochmaben, 1684. [LCC#179]

BYRES, JOHN, a resident of Lochmaben, 1642. [LCC#45]

BYRES, THOMAS, a resident of Lochmaben, 1642. [LCC#45]

BYRES, THOMAS, a bailie of Lochmaben, 1684. [LCC#179]

CADER, JOHN, a weaver in Dumfries, testament, 1688, Commissary of Dumfries. [NAS]

CAIMAN, JAMES, in Armainoch, parish of Lochrutton, 1620. [NAS.CS7/335]

CAIRD, ANDREW, in Woodend in the Bankend, parish of Caerlaverock, 1619. [NAS.CS7/335/109]

CAIRD, HERBERT, a merchant in Dumfries, relict Bessie Blackstock, testament, 1674, Commissary of Dumfries. [NAS]

CAIRD, JOHN, in Clachan of New Abbey, testament, 1641, Commissary of Dumfries. [NAS]

CAIRD, JOHN, a merchant in Dumfries, testament, 1674, Commissary of Dumfries. [NAS]

CAIRD, JOHN, in Kirkconnel town, testament, 1681, Commissary of Dumfries. [NAS]

CAIRD, JOHN, the younger, in Kennkerrock, testament, 1685, Commissary of Dumfries. [NAS]

CAIRNS, ADAM, in Lochrutton Gait, parish of Lochrutton, 1620. [NAS.CS7/335]

CAIRNS, HENRY, in Deanstoun, parish of Lochrutton, 1620. [NAS.CS7/335]

CAIRNS, HENRY, in Carsuada, parish of Lochrutton, 1620. [NAS.CS7.335.311]

CAIRNS, JOHN, in Staraheugh, testament, 1681, Commissary of Dumfries. [NAS]

CAIRNS, WILLIAM, and his wife Margaret Stott, testament, 1657, Commissary of Dumfries. [NAS]

CALLAN, JAMES, of Brockloch, spouse Marjorie Archibald, testament, 1686, Commissary of Dumfries. [NAS]

CALLAN, JOHN, of Brockloch, testaments, 1681, Commissary of Dumfries. [NAS]

CALLOW, THOMAS, in Dardarroch, testament, 1675, Commissary of Dumfries. [NAS]

CALVERT, JOHN, a merchant in Dumfries, 1621. [NAS.E71.10.5]

CAMMOCK, ADAM, in Ruchhill Croft, parish of Lochrutton, 1620. [NAS.CS7/335]

CAMMOCK, FERGUS, in Knockwalloch, testament, 1630, Commissary of Dumfries. [NAS]

CAMMOCK, JANET, in Dornald, parish of Balmaghie, 1619. [NAS.CS7/335/63]

CAMMOCK, JOHN, in Dornald, parish of Balmaghie, 1619. [NAS.CS7/335/63]

CAMMOCK, JOHN, in Felendcroft, parish of Lochrutton, 1620. [NAS.CS7/335]

CAMMOCK, RODGER, in Dornald, parish of Balmaghie, 1619. [NAS.CS7/335/63]

CAMPAND, GEORGE, in Brekoch, parish of Balmaghie, 1619. [NAS.CS7/335/63]

CAMPBELL, GEORGE, of Balserrach, parish of Kirkcolm, testament, 1600, Commissary of Edinburgh. [NAS]

CAMPBELL, GEORGE, born 1651, resident in Dungary, died 23 November 1706. [Buittle gravestone]

CAMPBELL, JOHN, of Loandornall, parish of Leswalt, testament, 1598, Commissary of Edinburgh. [NAS]

CAMPBELL, SAMUEL, master of the Marion of Dumfries, 1689. [NAS.E72.6.13]

CAMRELL. JOHN, at Greenhill, parish of Moffat, 1620. [NAS.CS7/335/265]

CAMRELL, ROBERT, in Hairhope, parish of Moffat, 1620. [NAS.CS7/335/265]

CANNON, SAMUEL, from Banscalloch, Kirkcudbright, a Covenanter banished to the American Plantations in 1684. [RPCS.X.144/177/229/258/377/604]

CARLISLE, ADAM, the elder, of Lymekills, testament, 1675, Commissary of Dumfries. [NAS]

CARLISLE, ADAM, late merchant in Annan, testament, 1686, Commissary of Dumfries. [NAS]

CARLISLE, AGNES, MARGARET, and JANET, heirs to their father William Carlisle a bailie burgess of Dumfries, 1658. [NAS,Retours, Dumfries#235]

CARLISLE, ALEXANDER, in Torthorwald, testament, 1657, Commissary of Dumfries. [NAS]

CARLISLE, JAMES, a merchant in Dumfries, 1677. [NAS.AC7/4]

CARLISLE, JOHN, in Kirkblane, parish of Caerlaverock, 1619. [NAS.CS7/335/109]

CARLISLE, JOHN, a merchant burgess of Dumfries, 1622; spouse Isobel Brown, testament, 1629, Commissary of Dumfries. [NAS.E71.10.5]

CARLISLE, JOHN, master of the Margaret of Dumfries, 1688-1691. [NAS.E72.6.13/18/24/25]

CARLISLE, WILLIAM, a merchant in Dumfries, trading with Flanders, 1622. [NAS.E71.10.5]

CARMICHAEL, ROBERT, a schoolmaster in Moffat, sought for the murder of a pupil, July 1699. [Edinburgh Gazette, 17.7.1699]

CARMONT, JOHN, a workman in Dumfries, testament, 1686, Commissary of Dumfries. [NAS]

CARMOUNT, ROBERT, in Urr, spouse Helen Hislop, testaments, 1624, Commissary of Dumfries. [NAS]

CARNIECROCE, JAMES, bailie of Sanquhar, testament, 1687, Commissary of Dumfries. [NAS]

CARNOCHAN, ALEXANDER, in Laggan, parish of Colven, testament, 1689, Commissary of Dumfries. [NAS]

CARNOCHAN, JOHN, in Smithland, parish of Colvend, testament, 1600, Commissary of Edinburgh. [NAS]

CARRICK, JANET, daughter of James Carrick, in Nether Ingliston, testament, 1689, Commissary of Dumfries. [NAS]

CARRUBERS, JAMES, in Broomhills, testament, 1657, Commissary of Dumfries. [NAS]

CARRUTHERS, AGNES, in Whitehills, Bordland of Coveine, testament, 1678, Commissary of Dumfries. [NAS]

CARRUTHERS, ANDREW, in Datonhook, parish of Dryfesdale, 1620. [NAS.CS7/335/294]

CARRUTHERS, ARCHIE, in the parish of Dryfesdale, 1620. [NAS.CS7/335/294]

CARRUTHERS, JAMES, in Datonhook, parish of Dryfesdale, 1620. [NAS.CS7/335/294]

CARRUTHERS, JOHN, in Lockerbie, parish of Dryfesdale, 1620. [NAS.CS7/335/294]

CARRUTHERS, JOHN, a resident of Lochmaben, 1642. [LCC#45]

CARRUTHERS, MARION, in Datonhook, parish of Dryfesdale, 1620. [NAS.CS7/335/294]

CARRUTHERS, ROBERT, of Ramerscales, a councillor of Lochmaben, 1684. [LCC#179]

CARRUTHERS, THOMAS, in Beckton, parish of Dryfesdale, 1620. [NAS.CS7/335/294]

CARRUTHERS, WILLIAM, a councillor of Lochmaben, 1684. [LCC#179]

CARSAN, CUTHBERT, at Gilligapok Mill, testament, 1626, Commissary of Dumfries. [NAS]

CARSAN, PATRICK, of Drummoir, testament, 1598, Commissary of Edinburgh. [NAS]

CARSAN, WILLIAM, in Carswada, parish of Lochrutton, 1620. [NAS.CS7/335]

CARSON, JOHN, born 1662, residing in Laggan, died 16 February 1734, his wife Jean Lowden, born 1681, died 12 March 1736. [Southwick gravestone]

CHALMERS, ANDREW, in Lockerbie, parish of Dryfesdale, 1620. [NAS.CS7/335/294]

CHALMERS, ANDREW, in Datonhook, parish of Dryfesdale, 1620. [NAS.CS7/335/294]

CHALMERS, ANDREW, the elder and the younger, in Tourmuir, parish of Dryfesdale, 1620. [NAS.CS7/335/294]

CHALMERS, BESSIE, in Behalhead, parish of Dryfesdale, 1620. [NAS.CS7/335/294]

CHALMERS, HEW, in Dun, parish of Dryfesdale, 1620. [NAS.CS7/335/294]

CHALMERS, HEW, in Dryisholme, parish of Dryfesdale, 1620. [NAS.CS7/335/294]

CHALMERS, JAMES, in Behalhead, parish of Dryfesdale, 1620. [NAS.CS7/335/294]

CHALMERS, JAMES, in Drysdalesgait, parish of Dryfesdale, 1620. [NAS.CS7/335/294]

CHALMERS, JOHN, in Behalhead, parish of Dryfesdale, 1620. [NAS.CS7/335/294]

CHALMERS JOHN, in Lockerbie, parish of Dryfesdale, 1620. [NAS.CS7/335/294]

CHALMERS, MATTHEW, in Behalhead, parish of Dryfesdale, 1620. [NAS.CS7/335/294]

CHALMERS, NINIAN, in Mantuarig, parish of Dryfesdale, 1620. [NAS.CS7/335/294]

CHALMERS, THOMAS, in Drysdalegait, parish of Dryfesdale, 1620. [NAS.CS7/335/294]

CHALMERS, WILLIAM, of Woodhead, parish of Kells, testament, 1598, Commissary of Edinburgh. [NAS]

CHALMERS, WILLIAM, in Dun, parish of Dryfesdale, 1620. [NAS.CS7/335/294]

CHARTERHOUSE, JAMES, of Kelwood, the younger, testament, 1596, Commissary of Edinburgh. [NAS]

CHARTERS, ARCHIBALD, in Barbachill, parish of Lochrutton, 1620. [NAS.CS7.335.311]

CHARTERS, GEORGE, in Thornhill, testament, 1688, Commissary of Dumfries. [NAS]

CHARTERS, JOHN, in Drumbrak, parish of Balmaghie, 1619. [NAS.CS7/335/63]

CHARTERS, JOHN, in Genocht, parish of Balmaghie, 1619. [NAS.CS7/335/63]

CHARTERS, ROBERT, of Kelwood, parish of Balmaghie, his wife Marion Gordon, testament, 1599, Commissary of Edinburgh. [NAS]

CHISHOLM, JOHN, at Kirkstyle of Ewes, testament, 1679, Commissary of Dumfries. [NAS]

CLARK, EDWARD, in Hills, parish of Lochrutton, 1620. [NAS.CS7/335]

CLARK, JOHN, in Nether Croft, parish of Lochrutton, 1620. [NAS.CS7/335]

CLARK, JOHN, in Carswada, parish of Lochrutton, 1620. [NAS.CS7/335]

CLARK, SIMON, in Killarne, testament, 1595, Commissary of Edinburgh. [NAS]

CLERK, ANDREW, from Lochrutten, Galloway, a Covenanter who was transported to Barbados in 1679, shipwrecked. [RBM]

CLERK, MARY, from Kirkcudbright, a Covenanter who was transported to Jamaica in 1685. [RPCS.IX.573/XI.329]

CLESPIK, JOHN, in Newlaw, parish of Rerrick, testament, 1595, Commissary of Edinburgh. [NAS]

COBHAM, THOMAS, a minister from Ireland in Dumfries-shire, 1689. [NAS.CH2.1284.2/39-48]

COCHRANE, ROBERT, in Knockinner, parish of Balmaghie, 1619. [NAS.CS7/335/63]

COKELL, RALPH, a resident of Lochmaben, 1642. [LCC#45]

COLIN, HENRY, in Beoch, testament, 1652, Commissary of Dumfries.

COLTART, JAMES, in Kidstone, testament, 1683, Commissary of Dumfries. [NAS]

COLTART, JOHN, in Westwood, testament, 1627, Commissary of Dumfries. [NAS]

COLTHERD, ROGER, in Cubbokes, testament, 1606, Commissary of Edinburgh. [NAS]

COLVILL, JAMES, from Glencairn, Nithsdale, a Covenanter who was transported to Barbados in 1679, shipwrecked. [RBM]

CONHAITH, JAMES, in Pairthet, spouse Nicola Blake, testament, 1763, Commissary of Dumfries. [NAS]

CONQUHIE, ALEXANDER, in Head, parish of Lochrutton, 1620. [NAS.CS7/335]

COOK, WILLIAM, in Nether Lauchcroft, testament, 1658, Commissary of Dumfries. [NAS]

COPLAND, JOHN, provost of Dumfries, testaments, 1687, 1688, Commissary of Dumfries. [NAS]

COPLAND, WILLIAM, heir to his father John Copland provost of Dumfries, 1687. [NAS.Retours, Dumfries#318]

CORBET, ADAM, a merchant burgess of Dumfries, testament, 1659, Commissary of Dumfries. [NAS]

CORBET, JOHN, a merchant burgess of Dumfries, testament, 1630, Commissary of Dumfries. [NAS]

CORREW, WILLIAM, in Knock, testament, 1673, Commissary of Dumfries. [NAS]

CORRIE, ARTHUR, in Crofthead, parish of Moffat, 1620; testament, 1630, Commissary of Dumfries. [NAS.CS7/335/265]

CORRIE, JOHN, in Brekoche, parish of Balmaghie, 1619. [NAS.CS7/335/63]

CORRIE, THOMAS, in Newbigging, parish of Moffat, 1620. [NAS.CS7/335/265]

CORRIE, THOMAS, in Glennae, testament, 1683, Commissary of Dumfries. [NAS]

CORSAN, GEORGE, a merchant burgess of Dumfries, spouse Bessie Young, testament, 1593, Commissary of Edinburgh. [NAS]

CORSAN, JAMES, from Kirkcudbrightshire, a Covenanter who was transported to Barbados in 1679, shipwrecked. [RBM]

CORSAN, JOHN, provost of Dumfries, 1619; testament, 1643, Commissary of Dumfries. [RPCS.XII.98]

CORSAN, JOHN, a Covenanter transported to East New Jersey in 1685. [RPCS.XI.154]

CORSAN, LAURENCE, from Glencairn, Dumfries-shire, a Covenanter banished to the American Plantations in 1684. [RPCS.X.311]

CORSAN, WILLIAM, in the parish of Lochrutton, 1620. [NAS.CS7.335.311]

CORSBIE, ANDREW, sr., a merchant burgess of Dumfries, testament, 1674, Commissary of Dumfries. [NAS]

CORSBIE, WILLIAM, in Blackshaw, parish of Caerlaverock, 1619. [NAS.CS7/335/109]

COSTAN, HUGH, a merchant in Dumfries, trading with Flanders, 1622. [NAS.E71.10.5]

COSTAN, ROBERT, in Burvane, spouse Janet Aitken, testament, 1676, Commissary of Dumfries. [NAS]

COULTER, JOHN, in Priestside, parish of Cummertrees, testaments, 1685, 1686, Commissary of Dumfries. [NAS]

COULTHART, JOHN, in County Wigtown, "chief of the name", born 1625, died 11 September 1690, his wife Janet Douglas, born 1628, died 24 June 1692, their son Robert was killed off St Vincent on 16 September 1693 fighting under Admiral Rooke, their son William, born 1658, died 9 November 1708. [Crossmichael gravestone]

COULTHART, RICHARD, of Coulthart, born 1659, died 10 November 1717, his wife Jean Gordon, born 1675, died 8 December 1730. [Crossmichael gravestone]

COWAN, ANDREW, former provost of Stranraer, co-owner of the Providence of Stranraer, 1675. [NAS.AC7/9]

COWAN, BARBARA, a Covenanter in Dumfries Tolbooth, transported to East New Jersey in 1685. [RPCS.XI.291]

COWAN, JOHN, in Dalswinton, testament, 1683, Commissary of Dumfries. [NAS]

CRAIK, EDWARD, in Torwood, parish of Dryfesdale, 1620. [NAS.CS7/335/294]

CRAIK, JAMES, of Stewarton, heir to his father John Craik a bailie and merchant in Dumfries, 1643; testament, 1687, Commissary of Dumfries. [NAS.Retours, Dumfries#177]

CRAIK, JOHN, in Broomhouse, parish of Dryfesdale, 1620. [NAS.CS7/294]

CRAIK, JOHN, a merchant in Dumfries, trading with Flanders, 1622. [NAS.E71.10.5]

CRAIK, MATTHEW, in Broomhouse, parish of Dryfesdale, 1620. [NAS.CS7/335/294]

CRAIK, ROBERT, in Glengaber, parish of Holywood, testament, 1600, Commissary of Dumfries. [NAS]

CRAWFORD, JOHN, of Beircroft, Dumfries-shire, was enrolled as an Undertaker for the Plantation of Ulster with a grant of 2000 acres in 1609. [RPCS.VIII.329]

CREICHTON, DAVID, in Datonhook, parish of Dryfesdale, 1620. [NAS.CS7/335/294]

CREICHTON, JANET, in Datonhook, parish of Dryfesdale, 1620. [NAS.CS7/335/294]

CREICHTON, JOHN, in Overbyres, parish of Dryfesdale, 1620. [NAS.CS7/335/294]

CREICHTON, JOHN, elder and younger, in Datonhook, parish of Dryfesdale, 1620. [NAS.CS7/335/294]

CREICHTON, NINIAN, in Datonhook, parish of Dryfesdale, 1620. [NAS.CS7/335/294]

CREICHTON, THOMAS, in Datonhook, parish of Dryfesdale, 1620. [NAS.CS7/335/294]

CREICHTON, WILLIAM, of Ryhill, 1614. [CLC#1702]

CRICHTON, GEORGE, in Blaiket, parish of Urr, testament, 1642, Commissary of Dumfries. [NAS]

CRICHTON, MUNGO, in Kilnair, parish of Dalry, spouse Christian Grierson, testament, 1598, Commissary of Edinburgh. [NAS]

CRICHTON, ROBERT, in Carne, parish of Kirkconnell, testament, 1590, Commissary of Edinburgh. [NAS]

CRICHTON, ROBERT, of Carco, parish of Sanquhar, testament, 1599, Commissary of Edinburgh. [NAS]

CROCKETT, GILBERT, in Holmes, parish of Troqueeer, testament, 1595, Commissary of Edinburgh. [NAS]

CROCKETT, GILBERT, in Hall of Barquhar, parish of Lochrutton, 1620. [NAS.CS7/335]

CROCKETT, GILBERT, a merchant in Dumfries, spouse Marion Blacklock, testaments, 1687, 1693, Commissary of Dumfries; relict Mary, daughter of John McMichan of Barcaple, deed, 1696. [NAS.RD2.79.795]

CROCKETT, HARBERT, in Hills, parish of Lochrutton, 1620. [NAS.CS7/335]

CROCKETT, HERBERT, in Kirkconnell town, testament, 1680, Commissary of Dumfries. [NAS]

CROCKETT, JOHN, a merchant in Dumfries, spouse Mary Newlands, deed, 1699. [NAS.RD4.85.87]

CROCKETT, PETER, in Hills, parish of Lochrutton, 1620. [NAS.CS7/335]

CRUSTEIN, MARION, in Prestane, testament, 1657, Commissary of Dumfries. [NAS]

CUBBIN, WILLIAM, in Meikle Duchray, parish of Balmaghie, 1619. [NAS.CS7/335/63]

CUBBIN, WILLIAM, in Greenhead, parish of Caerlaverock, 1619. [NAS.CS7/335/109]

CULZEAN, JOHN, in Sherington, parish of Caerlaverock, 1619. [NAS.CS7/335/109]

CUMING, ANDREW, in Fuldoris, parish of Dryfesdale, 1620. [NAS.CS7/335/294]

CUNNINGHAM, ALEXANDER, of Powton, Sorbie, Wigtownshire, was enrolled as an Undertaker for the Plantation of Ulster with a grant of 2000 acres in 1609. [RPCS.VIII.329]; an Undertaker in County Donegal, 1611. [Cal.SP.Ire.1611/384]

CUNNINGHAM, CUTHBERT, in Castle Fairn, testament, 1598, Commissary of Edinburgh. [NAS]

CUNNINGHAM, GEORGE, a priest in Shaw, parish of Glencairn, testament, 1591, Commissary of Edinburgh. [NAS]

CUNNINGHAM, JAMES, in Creichan, testament, 1686, Commissary of Dumfries. [NAS]

CUNNINGHAM, WILLIAM, in Lincluden, testament, 1596, Commissary of Edinburgh. [NAS]

CURRIE, HERBERT, in St Mungo, testament, 1657, Commissary of Dumfries. [NAS]

CURROR, JOHN, minister of Lochrutton, 1620. [NAS.CS7/335]

CURROR, MARGARET, in Hall of Barquhar, parish of Lochrutton, 1620. [NAS.CS7/335]

CURROR, PETER, in parish of Kirkpatrick-Irongray, testament, 1624, Commissary of Dumfries. [NAS]

CURROW, ANDREW, a merchant in Dumfries, testament, 1686, Commissary of Dumfries. [NAS]

CUTHBERTSON, JOHN, in Hoddom, testament, 1657, Commissary of Dumfries. [NAS]

CUTLER, ARCHIBALD, heir to his father John Cutler of Orroland, 1700. [NAS.Retours. Kirkcudbright#394]

CUTTER, JOHN, sr., in Oldwickpool, testament, 1658, Commissary of Dumfries. [NAS]

DALGLEISH, JOHN, in Moss-side, spouse Janet Beattie, testament, 1684, Commissary of Dumfries. [NAS]

DALGLEISH, WALTER, minister at Westerkirk, testament, 1688, Commissary of Dumfries. [NAS]

DALRYMPLE, JAMES, in Keir Mill, testament, 1658, Commissary of Dumfries. [NAS]

DALRYMPLE, MALCOLM, of Waterside, testament, 1624, Commissary of Dumfries. [NAS]

DALYELL, Sir JOHN, of Glennae, testament, 1691, Commissary of Dumfries. [NAS]

DALYELL, WILLIAM, in Craigdarroch, testament, 1627, Commissary of Dumfries. [NAS]

DALZELL, JAMES, in Glengairn, spouse Agnes Broadfoot, testament, 1638, Commissary of Dumfries. [NAS]

DAVIDSON, ANDREW, in Balfill, parish of Lochrutton, 1620. [NAS.CS7.335.311]

DAVIDSON, ANDREW, and his mother Margaret Johnston, in the parish of Moffat, 1620. [NAS.CS7/335/265]

DAVIDSON, JOHN, in the parish of Moffat, 1620. [NAS.CS7/335/265]

DAVIDSON, PETER, in Closeburn, testament, 1658, Commissary of Dumfries. [NAS]

DAVIDSON, ROBERT, a miller in Clowden, testament, 1688, Commissary of Dumfries. [NAS]

DAVIDSON, THOMAS, in Meikleholmside, parish of Moffat, 1620. [NAS.CS7/335/265]

DEANS, GEORGE, a notary in Penfillan, testaments, 1675, 1691, Commissary of Dumfries. [NAS]

DENHOLM, DAVID, of Criechen, testament, 1629, Commissary of Dumfries. [NAS]

DICKSON, ADAM, a barber burgess of Dumfries, testament, 1678, Commissary of Dumfries. [NAS]

DICKSON, ALEXANDER, in Hemayns, parish of Caerlaverock, 1619. [NAS.CS7/335/109]

DICKSON, CLEMENT, parish of Caerlaverock, 1619. [NAS.CS7/335/109]

DICKSON, GEORGE, spouse Janet Byres, testament, 1657, Commissary of Dumfries. [NAS]

DICKSON, HARBERT, a resident of Lochmaben, 1642. [LCC#45]

DICKSON, HENDRY, a resident of Lochmaben, 1642. [LCC#45]

DICKSON, JAMES, a resident of Lochmaben, 1642. [LCC#45]

DICKSON, JOHN, parish of Caerlaverock, 1619. [NAS.CS7/335/109]

DICKSON, JOHN, in Blackshaw, parish of Caerlaverock, 1619. [NAS.CS7/335/109]

DICKSON, JOHN, an officer in Sherington, parish of Caerlaverock, 1619. [NAS.CS7/335/109]

DICKSON, JOHN, a merchant in Dumfries, 1621. [NAS.E71.10.5]

DICKSON, JOHN, the younger, a councillor of Lochmaben, 1684. [LCC#179]

DICKSON, JOHN, a shoemaker in Lockerbie, and spouse Elizabeth Stitt, deed, 1697. [NAS.RD3.87.84]

DICKSON, MARTIN, in Lockerbie, parish of Dryfesdale, 1620. [NAS.CS7/ 335/294]

DICKSON, NINIAN, Dean of Guild in Sanquhar, testament, 1684, Commissary of Dumfries. [NAS]

DICKSON, ROBERT, in Keltoun, testament, 1598, Commissary of Edinburgh. [NAS]

DICKSON, THOMAS, in the parish of Caerlaverock, 1619. [NAS.CS7/335/ 109]

DICKSON, THOMAS, in Tourmuir, parish of Dryfesdale, 1620. [NAS.CS7/ 335/294]

DICKSON, THOMAS, a resident of Lochmaben, 1642. [LCC#45]

DICKSON, WILLIAM, in Blackshaw, parish of Caerlaverock, 1619. [NAS.CS7/335/109]

DICKSON, WILLIAM, in Tourmuir, parish of Dryfesdale, 1620. [NAS.CS7/ 335/294]

DIN, THOMAS, in Glencaple, parish of Caerlaverock, testament, 1639, Commissary of Dumfries. [NAS]

DINWIDDIE, JOHN, in Moss-side, testament, 1656, Commissary of Dumfries. [NAS]

DINWIDDIE, JOHN, a merchant in Dunreggan, testament, 1682, Commissary of Dumfries. [NAS]

DOBBIE, JOHN, in Lockerbie, testament, 1679, Commissary of Dumfries. [NAS]

DOBBIE, THOMAS, in Mantuarig, parish of Dryfesdale, 1620. [NAS.CS7/335/294]

DOBBIE, THOMAS, in Kirkton of Dryfesdale, deed, 1697. [NAS.RD4.81.366]

DOBBIE, WILLIAM, in Dryisholme, parish of Dryfesdale, 1620. [NAS.CS7/335/294]

DODDS, ANDREW, a resident of Lochmaben, 1642. [LCC#45]

DONALDSON, ALEXANDER, master of the Anne of Kirkcudbright, 1673. [NAS.E72.6.2]

DONALDSON, ANDREW, from Girthorn, Kirkcudbrightshie, a Covenanter who was transported to Barbados in 1679, shipwrecked. [RBM]

DONALDSON, DAVID, born 1671, resident of Darscob, died 28 April 1728. [Balmaclellan gravestone]

DONALDSON, JAMES, from Kelton, Kirkcudbrightshie, a Covenanter who was transported to Barbados in 1679, shipwrecked. [RBM]

DONALDSON, RICHARD, in Whiteyard, testament, 1624, Commissary of Dumfries. [NAS]

DOUGLAS, DUNCAN, in Glenshalloch, spouse Mallie Gordon, testament, 1598, Commissary of Edinburgh. [NAS]

DOUGLAS, GEORGE, in Almernes, parish of Buittle, testament, 1591, Commissary of Edinburgh. [NAS]

DOUGLAS, JAMES, tacksman of Lochrutton, 1620. [NAS.CS7/335]

DOUGLAS, JAMES, a stabler burgess of Dumfries, testament, 1684, Commissary of Dumfries. [NAS]

DOUGLAS, JOHN, in Newton, Dumfries, spouse Janet Porter, testament, 1590, Commissary of Edinburgh. [NAS]

DOUGLAS, JOHN, of Arcland, parish of Penpont, spouse Katherine Stewart, testament, 1599, Commissary of Edinburgh. [NAS]

DOUGLAS, WILLIAM, in Scroggiehill, parish of Durrisdeer, testament, 1599, Commissary of Edinburgh. [NAS]

DOUGLAS, WILLIAM, of Drumlanrig, provost of Lincluden College, 1616. [CLC#1757]

DRONNAN, JOHN, tenant in Kirklebryde, testament, 1681, Commissary of Dumfries. [NAS]

DRYFFE, JOHN, in Hurlebus, parish of Kirkconnell, testament, 1641, Commissary of Dumfries. [NAS]

DRYSDALE, JOHN, in Littlequarter, testament, 1659, Commissary of Dumfries. [NAS]

DRYSDALE, THOMAS, testament, 1658, Commissary of Dumfries. [NAS]

DUNBAR, ALEXANDER, of Egines, Wigtownshire, was enrolled as an Undertaker for the Plantation of Ulster with a grant of 2000 acres in 1609. [RPCS.VIII.317]

DUNBAR, JOHN, in Orchardton, parish of Kirkmaiden, testament, 1599, Commissary of Edinburgh. [NAS]

DUNBAR, MARGARET, arrived in Dumfries during 1690 from Ireland. [NAS.CH2.537.15.1/34]

DUNBAR, PATRICK, of Crawlaw, parish of Mochrum, spouse Katherine Kennedy, testament, 1600, Commissary of Edinburgh. [NAS]

DUNCAN, PETER, in Hills, parish of Lochrutton, 1620. [NAS.CS7/335]

DUNGALLSON, JOHN, in Culmen, testament, 1627, Commissary of Dumfries. [NAS]

DUNN, JOHN, in Glencaple, parish of Caerlaverock, 1619. [NAS.CS7/335/109]

DUNN, JOHN, in Blackshaw, testament, 1685, Commissary of Dumfries. [NAS]

DUNN, MARION, in Blackshaw, parish of Caerlaverock, 1619. [NAS.CS7/335/109]

DUNN, MATTHEW, in the parish of Caerlaverock, 1619. [NAS.CS7/335/109]

DUNN, RODGER, born 1659 in Benwhat, Dalmellington, a Covenanter who was killed on Brockloch farm in June 1689. [Carsphairn gravestone]

DUNN, THOMAS, in Glencaple, parish of Caerlaverock, 1619. [NAS.CS7/335/109]

DUNN, WILLIAM, in Glencaple, parish of Caerlaverock, 1619. [NAS.CS7/335/109]

DURHAM, ELSPETH, in Moss-side, testament, 1683, Commissary of Dumfries. [NAS]

DURHAM, JOHN, in Dinance, parish of Balmaghie, 1619. [NAS.CS7/335/63]

EDGAR, ANDREW, a burgess of Dumfries, testament, 1592, Commissary of Edinburgh. [NAS]

EDGAR, ANDREW, of Guliehill, parish of Holywood, testament, 1592, Commissary of Edinburgh. [NAS]

EDGAR, BESSIE, in Bourlands, parish of Caerlaverock, 1619. [NAS.CS7/335/109]

EDGAR, DAVID, of Guliehill, parish of Holywood, testament, 1590, Commissary of Edinburgh. [NAS]

EDGAR, DAVID, heir to his sister Christine, re lands in parish of Holywood, 1602. [NAS.Retours.Dumfries#14]

EDGAR, DAVID, a merchant burgess of Dumfries, testament, 1685, Commissary of Dumfries. [NAS]

EDGAR, EDWARD, in Glenhowen, parish of Caerlaverock, 1619. [NAS.CS7/335/109]

EDGAR, HALBERT, master of the John of Kirkcudbright, 1673. [NAS.E72.16.2]

EDGAR, JOHN, master of the Anne of Kirkcudbright, 1673. [NAS.E72.6.2]

EDGAR, JOHN, Deacon of the Squaremen of Dumfries, testament, 1684, Commissary of Dumfries. [NAS]

EDGAR, JOHN, in Hemayns, parish of Caerlaverock, 1619. [NAS.CS7/335/109]

EDGAR, JOHN, in Lands, parish of Caerlaverock, 1619. [NAS.CS7/335/109]

EDGAR, JOHN, in Carmuck, parish of Caerlaverock, 1619. [NAS.CS7/335/109]

EDGAR, JOHN, from Barmaclellan, Kirkcudbrightshie, a Covenanter who was transported to Barbados in 1679, shipwrecked. [RBM]

EDGAR, JOHN, from Dumfries, a member of the Scots Charitable Society of Boston in 1694. [NEHGS/SCS]

EDGAR, MATTHEW, in Bowhouse, parish of Caerlaverock, 1619. [NAS.CS7/335/109]

EDGAR, NICOLL, in Carmuck, parish of Caerlaverock, 1619. [NAS.CS7/ 335/109]

EDGAR, ROBERT, in Bankend, parish of Caerlaverock, 1619. [NAS.CS7/ 335/109]

EDGAR, ROBERT, of the Woodend in the Bankend, parish of Caerlaverock, 1619. [NAS.CS7/335/109]

EDGAR, ROBERT, in Bowhouse, parish of Caerlaverock, 1619. [NAS.CS7/ 335/109]

EDGAR, THOMAS, in Sherington, parish of Caerlaverock, 1619. [NAS.CS7/ 335/109]

EDGAR, THOMAS, in Bankend, parish of Caerlaverock, 1619. [NAS.CS7/ 335/109]

EDGAR, WILLIAM, in Sherington, parish of Caerlaverock, 1619. [NAS.CS7/ 335/109]

EDGAR, WILLIAM, in Blackshaw, parish of Caerlaverock, 1619. [NAS.CS7/ 335/109]

EDGAR, WILLIAM, in Woodend of Bankend; parish of Caerlaverock, 1619. [NAS.CS7/335/109]

EDMISTOUN, JAMES, a merchant in Dumfries, 1621. [NAS.E71.10.5]

ELDER, JOHN, in Glenhowen, parish of Caerlaverock, 1619. [NAS.CS7/ 335/109]

ELDER, WILLIAM, in Glenhowen, parish of Caerlaverock, 1619. [NAS.CS7/ 335/109]

ELLIOT, ADAM, in Meikledale, testament, 1684, Commissary of Dumfries. [NAS]

ELLIOT, ADAM, in Cannobie Mill, testament, 1684, Commissary of Dumfries. [NAS]

ERLE, ANDREW, in Datonhook, parish of Dryfesdale, 1620. [NAS.CS7/335/294]

ESKDALE, JOHN, in Nether Dallsible, testament, 1674, Commissary of Dumfries. [NAS]

ESPIE, JOHN, in Ingliston, testament, 1673, Commissary of Dumfries. [NAS]

EWART, ADAM, in Emsbank, parish of Moffat, 1620. [NAS.CS7/335/265]

EWART, JAMES, in Corhead, parish of Moffat, 1620. [NAS.CS7/335/265]

EWART, JOHN, from Kirkcudbright, a freeholder in Ulster, 1620s. [NAS.RH15.91.33]

EWART, JOHN, the elder, in Preston, spouse Mally Briggs, testament, 1675, Commissary of Dumfries. [NAS]

EWART, PATRICK, a resident of Lochmaben, 1642. [LCC#45]

EWART, ROBERT, in Corhead, parish of Moffat, 1620. [NAS.CS7/335/265]

EWART, WILLIAM, a resident of Lochmaben, 1642. [LCC#45]

FAIRIES, DAVID, in Woodhouse, testament, 1686, Commissary of Dumfries. [NAS]

FAIRIES, JAMES, a tailor burgess of Dumfries, testament, 1674, Commissary of Dumfries. [NAS]

FARRIS, ADAM, in Over Mossop, parish of Moffat, 1620. [NAS.CS7/335/265]

FAULDS, ARCHIBALD, born around 1674 in Inveraray, a soldier who fought in Flanders and Germany in the service of King William, later a gardener at Bardarroch from 1703 to 1719, husband of Mary Campbell, parents of William, Archibald, Nicholas, John, Archibald, and David, died at Woodend in August 1724. [Anwoth gravestone]

FAW, ALEXANDER, a vagabond and robber in Annandale, to be caught and transported to the American Colonies, 1671. [RPCS.III.428]

FAW, HENRY, a vagabond and robber in Annandale, to be caught and transported to the American Colonies, 1671. [RPCS.III.428]

FAW, NINIAN, a vagabond and robber in Annandale, to be caught and transported to the American Colonies, 1671. [RPCS.III.428]

FAW, ROBERT, a vagabond and robber in Annandale, to be caught and transported to the American Colonies, 1671. [RPCS.III.428]

FAW, THOMAS, a vagabond and robber in Annandale, to be caught and transported to the American Colonies, 1671. [RPCS.III.428]

FAW, WILLIAM, a vagabond and robber in Annandale, to be caught and transported to the American Colonies, 1671. [RPCS.III.428]

FEAD, JOHN, at the Kirk of Holywood, testament, 1657, Commissary of Dumfries. [NAS]

FELL, JAMES, miller at Sandbed Mill, testament, 1628, Commissary of Dumfries. [NAS]

FERGUSON, EDWARD, servant to Robert Douglas provost of Lincluden, testament, 1600, Commissary of Edinburgh. [NAS]

FERGUSON, JAMES, a merchant councillor of Lochmaben, 1684. [LCC#179]

FERGUSON, JANET, daughter of the late Cuthbert Ferguson in Corrowdour, parish of Glencairn, testament, 1591, Commissary of Edinburgh. [NAS]

FERGUSON, JOHN, in Sherington, parish of Caerlaverock, 1619. [NAS.CS7/335/109]

FERGUSON, JOHN, from Glencairn, Dumfries-shire, a Covenanter who was transported to Barbados in 1679, shipwrecked. [RBM]

FERGUSON, MALCOLM, in Ketloch, parish of Glencairn, testament, 1592, Commissary of Edinburgh. [NAS]

FERGUSON, WILLIAM, in Ferington, relict Janet Caird, testament, 1674, Commissary of Dumfries. [NAS]

FERGUSON, WILLIAM, from Glencairn, Nithsdale, Dumfries-shire, a Covenanter who was transported to Barbados in 1679, shipwrecked. [RBM]

FINGLASS, WILLIAM, a bailie of Dumfries, testament, 1687, Commissary of Dumfries. [NAS]

FIRSHALL, WILLIAM, of Little Locklax, testament, 1675, Commissary of Dumfries. [NAS]

FISHER, EDWARD, arrived in Dumfries during 1690 from Ireland. [NAS.CH2.537.15.1/29]

FISHER, WILLIAM, a burgess of Sanquhar, testament, 1675, Commissary of Dumfries. [NAS]

FITT, JOHN, in Hoil, testament, 1657, Commissary of Dumfries. [NAS]

FLECK, ROBERT, a cooper, spouse Margaret Adamson, testament, 1679, Commissary of Dumfries. [NAS]

FLEMING, WILLIAM, in Carcasse, parish of Sanquhar, testaments, 1640, 1641, Commissary of Dumfries. [NAS]

FORRESTER, ROBERT, the elder, a burgess of Kirkcudbright, spouse Janet Houstoun, testament, 1591, Commissary of Edinburgh. [NAS]

FORRESTER, WILLIAM, of Kidisdale, parish of Glasserton, testament, 1599, Commissary of Edinburgh. [NAS]

FORSYTH, EDWARD, in Torthorwald, testament, 1659, Commissary of Dumfries. [NAS]

FORSYTH, JAMES, from Annandale, a Covenanter transported to East New Jersey in 1685. [RPCS.XI.154/291]

FORSYTH, JOHN, parish of Caerlaverock, 1619. [NAS.CS7/335/109]

FORSYTH, JOHN, in Hemayins, parish of Caerlaverock, 1619. [NAS.CS7/335/109]

FORSYTH, JOHN, in Glenhowen, parish of Caerlaverock, 1619. [NAS.CS7/335/109]

FORSYTH, PETER, a merchant in Dumfries, 1621. [NAS.E71.10.5]

FRASER, ALEXANDER, in Dincow, testament, 1679, Commissary of Dumfries. [NAS]

FRASER, DAVID, a merchant burgess of Dumfries, testament, 1642, Commissary of Dumfries. [NAS]

FRASER, GILBERT, in Schang, parish of Mochrum, spouse Marjory Maxwell, testament, 1598, Commissary of Edinburgh. [NAS]

FRASER, JOHN, a schoolmaster in Dumfries, deed, 1684. [NAS.RD4.53.816]

FRENCH, ADAM, in Logan, parish of Moffat, 1620. [NAS.CS7/335/265]

FRENCH, ADAM, in Giddishaw, testament, 1688, Commissary of Dumfries. [NAS]

FRENCH, BESSIE, in the parish of Moffat, 1620. [NAS.CS7/335/265]

FRENCH, DAVID, in the parish of Moffat, 1620. [NAS.CS7/335/265]

FRENCH, EDWARD, in the parish of Moffat, 1620. [NAS.CS7/335/265]

FRENCH, JOHN, in Erectstane, parish of Moffat, 1620. [NAS.CS7/335/265]

FRENCH, ROBERT, of Mot, parish of Moffat, 1620. [NAS.CS7/335/265]

FRENCH, ROBERT, a merchant from Kilpatrick, Annandale, a member of the Scots Charitable Society of Boston in 1685. [NEHGS/SCS]

FRENCH, THOMAS, of Auldhousehill, parish of Moffat, 1620. [NAS.CS7/335/265]

FRENCH, WILLIAM, of Frenchland, parish of Moffat, 1620. [NAS.CS7/335/265]

FRENCH, WILLIAM, heir to his mother Margaret Johnston spouse of David French in Frenchland, 1635. [NAS.Retours, Dumfries#157]

FRESCHIE, CUTHBERT, in Burnside of Baltersen, testament, 1659, Commissary of Dumfries. [NAS]

FRUID, JOHN, and his spouse Janet Dickson in Blackshaw, testament, 1657, Commissary of Dumfries. [NAS]

FULLARTON, JOHN, in Kirkconnell, testament, 1596, Commissary of Edinburgh. [NAS]

FULLARTON, Lieutenant Colonel JOHN, of Sennick, testament, 1694, Commissary of Edinburgh. [NAS]

FURMONT, ROBERT, a maltman burgess of Dumfries, testament, 1638, Commissary of Dumfries. [NAS]

GALLOWAY, ARCHIBALD, in Gairland, testament, 1659, Commissary of Dumfries. [NAS]

GALLOWAY, JOHN, a wauker in Nether Kilqhuannadie, testament, 1674, Commissary of Dumfries. [NAS]

GASS, JOHN, in Tordoch, testament, 1626, Commissary of Dumfries. [NAS]

GASS, THOMAS, in Dornock, testament, 1693, Commissary of Dumfries. [NAS]

GEIR, GEORGE, a burgess of Dumfries, spouse Jane Bell, testament, 1600, Commissary of Edinburgh. [NAS]

GELLIE, WILLIAM, a merchant in Dumfries, 1621. [NAS.E71.10.5]

GIBSON, ADAM, in Raecleuch, parish of Moffat, 1620. [NAS.CS7/335/265]

GIBSON, ANDREW, in Glenhowen, parish of Caerlaverock, 1619. [NAS.CS7/335/109]

GIBSON, CHARLES, in Glenhowen, parish of Caerlaverock, 1619. [NAS.CS7/335/109]

GIBSON, CLEMENT, in Sherington, parish of Caerlaverock, 1619. [NAS.CS7/335/109]

GIBSON, JANET, a widow in Dumfries, testament, 1597, Commissary of Edinburgh. [NAS]

GIBSON, R., died 6 November 1683. [Carsphairn gravestone]

GIBSON, THOMAS, master of the Fleshers of Dumfries, 1661. [DAC]

GIBSON, WILLIAM, in Sherington, parish of Caerlaverock, 1619. [NAS.CS7/335/109]

GILCHRIST, BETTY, from Kilroy, Dumfries-shire, a Covenanter banished to the American Plantations in 1684. [RPCS.X.309/377/562/570/578/587]

GILCHRIST, JOHN, in Porterston, testament, 1680, Commissary of Dumfries. [NAS]

GILCHRIST, ROBERT, from Dalgarnock, Nithsdale, a Covenanter transported to East New Jersey in 1685. [RPCS.XI.154//290/292][NAS.RD4.83.421]

GILCHRIST, THOMAS, a merchant in Dumfries, 1622. [NAS.E71.10.5]

GILLESPIE, JOHN, minister at Lochrutton, testament, 1683, Commissary of Dumfries. [NAS]

GILLESPIE, PETER, in Potthouse, testament, 1625, Commissary of Dumfries. [NAS]

GILLISON, ROBERT, in Cloudon, testament, 1685, Commissary of Dumfries. [NAS]

GILMUIR, ROBERT, in Bruntskarth, testament, 1690, Commissary of Dumfries. [NAS]

GLASSELL, JOHN, in Ruken, testament, 1657, Commissary of Dumfries. [NAS]

GLEDSTONES, HERBERT, burgess of Kirkcudbright, spouse Marion Dalziel, testament, 1594, Commissary of Edinburgh. [NAS]

GLEDSTANES, HERBERT, in Knockfernoch, testament, 1599, Commissary of Edinburgh. [NAS]

GLEDSTANES, JOHN, parish of Caerlaverock, 1619. [NAS.CS7/335/109]

GLENCORSE, THOMAS, a merchant in Dumfries, 1621; testament, 1626, Commissary of Dumfries. [NAS.E71.10.5]

GLENDENNING, ADAM, in Corheid, parish of Moffat, 1620. [NAS.CS7/335/265]

GLENDENNING, ALEXANDER, of Drumrash, and spouse Marion McGhie, deed, 1697. [NAS.RD4.80.1409]

GLENDENNING, ISOBEL, in Greenknow, parish of Dryfesdale, 1620. [NAS.CS7/335/294]

GLENDENNING, JOHN, in Penninghame, testament, 1593, Commissary of Edinburgh. [NAS]

GLENDENNING, JOHN, in Bordland of Garleis, parish of Minnigaff, testament, 1599, Commissary of Edinburgh. [NAS]

GLENDENNING, NINIAN, in the parish of Moffat, 1620. [NAS.CS7/335/265]

GLENDENNING, WILLIAM, a merchant in Dumfries, 1621. [NAS.E71.10.5]

GLENDENNING, WILLIAM, Customs controller of Kirkcudbright, 1639-1641. [NAS.E73.9.7]

GLENDYNING, JOHN, of Drumrasche, testament, 1611, Commissary of Edinburgh. [NAS]

GLOVER, WILLIAM, in Castle Robert, testament, 1630, Commissary of Dumfries. [NAS]

GOLDIE, JAMES, a flesher burgess of Dumfries, testament, 1685, Commissary of Dumfries. [NAS]

GOLDIE, JOHN, was appointed schoolmaster of Moffat, Dumfries-shire, in 1663. [Edinburgh Burgh Records, 15.5.1663]

GOLDIE, THOMAS, a merchant burgess of Dumfries, testament, 1638, Commissary of Dumfries. [NAS]

GOOD, ROBERT, at the Bridgend of Dumfries, testament, 1687, Commissary of Dumfries. [NAS]

GORDON, ALEXANDER, of Barncrum, parish of Tongland, testament, 1590, Commissary of Edinburgh. [NAS]

GORDON, ALEXANDER, of Barkeoch, parish of Kirkmaiden, spouse Jane Crawford, testament, 1598, Commissary of Edinburgh. [NAS]

GORDON, ALEXANDER, in Knockbrax, his wife Janet McClellan, testament, 1601, Commissary of Edinburgh. [NAS]

GORDON, ANDREW, in Tannyford, spouse Janet Lennox, testament, 1598, Commissary of Edinburgh. [NAS]

GORDON, JAMES, of Barnbarroch, parish of Colvend, spouse Agnes McClellan, testament, 1592, Commissary of Edinburgh. [NAS]

GORDON, JAMES, a merchant in Dumfries, deed, 1697. [NAS.RD4.80.143]

GORDON, JEAN, born 1661, died 1695. [Balmaclellan gravestone]

GORDON, JOHN, a merchant in Glenluce, testament, 1595, Commissary of Edinburgh. [NAS]

GORDON, Sir JOHN, of Airds, spouse Margaret Sinclair, testament, 1596, Commissary of Edinburgh. [NAS]

GORDON, JOHN, of Balskeoch, parish of Kirkmaiden, testament, 1598, Commissary of Edinburgh. [NAS]

GORDON, JOHN, in Barley, testament, 1607, Commissary of Edinburgh. [NAS]

GORDON, JOHN, of Slogarie, parish of Balmaghie, 1619. [NAS.CS7/335/63]

GORDON, JOHN, of Kirkconnell, deeds, 1697. [NAS.RD2.81/1.120]

GORDON, JOHN, a dyer at the Bridgend of Dumfries, deed, 1697. [NAS.RD4.81.1439]

GORDON, JOHN, of Auchendolle, born 1658, died 28 October 1708, his wife Janet Maxwell, born 1658, died 13 February 1734. [Crossmichael gravestone]

GORDON, MARGARET, from Arioland, Wigtownshire, a Covenanter banished to the American Plantations in 1684. [RPCS.X.606/608/610/612]

GORDON, ROBERT, in Park, parish of Kells, testament, 1594, Commissary of Edinburgh. [NAS]

GORDON, ROBERT, in the Forrest of Bothane, spouse Bessie McKie, testament, 1592, Commissary of Edinburgh. [NAS]

GORDON, ROBERT, in Knockgray, his wife Margaret McAdam, testament, 1601, Commissary of Edinburgh. [NAS]

GORDON, Sir ROBERT, of Lochinvar, was granted lands in Donegal, 1616. [CLC#1739/1757]

GORDON, ROGER, of Schirmers, testament, 1596, Commissary of Edinburgh. [NAS]

GORDON, ROGER, minister of Whithorn, parish of Kirkinnar, his widow Janet Stewart, testament, 1598, Commissary of Edinburgh. [NAS]

GORDON, THOMAS, in Torris of Glenluce, testament, 1595, Commissary of Edinburgh. [NAS]

GORDON, WILLIAM, in Kilstire, parish of Sorbie, spouse Janet Gordon, testament, 1590, Commissary of Edinburgh. [NAS]

GORDON, WILLIAM, in Knockingarroch, parish of Carsphairn, deed, 1697. [NAS.RD2.80/2.117]

GORDON, WILLIAM, of Holm, born 1644, died 7 September 1714, his wife Jean Gordon, born 1651, died 9 January 1721. [Balmaclellan gravestone]

GORDON, WILLIAM, of Shirmers, born 1652, died 24 January 1717. [Balmaclellan gravestone]

GOURLAY, JANET, in Thrid, parish of Lochrutton, 1620. [NAS.CS7/335]

GOURLAY, THOMAS, a burgess of Dumfries, testament, 1629, Commissary of Dumfries. [NAS]

GRACIE, ALEXANDER, in Corridowe, testament, 1679, Commissary of Dumfries. [NAS]

GRACIE, CHRISTIAN, in Penpont, testament, 1627, Commissary of Dumfries. [NAS]

GRAHAM, ANDREW, in Lockerbie, parish of Dryfesdale, 1620. [NAS.CS7/335/294]

GRAHAM, ARCHIE, in Corilaw, parish of Drydesdale, 1620. [NAS.CS7/335/294]

GRAHAM, ARCHIE, in Coopwood, parish of Dryfesdale, 1620. [NAS.CS7/335/294]

GRAHAM, GEORGE, in Coopwood, parish of Dryfesdale, 1620. [NAS.CS7/335/294]

GRAHAM, GEORGE, a merchant in Dumfries, 1621. [NAS.E71.10.5]

GRAHAM, JAMES, in Corilaw, parish of Drydesdale, 1620. [NAS.CS7/335/294]

GRAHAM, JAMES, in Berneston, his widow Isobel Anderson, testament, 1686, Commissary of Dumfries. [NAS]

GRAHAM, or REID, JANET, born 1633, died 7 June 1714. [Carsphairn gravestone]

GRAHAM, JOHN, in Auchendoley, testament, 1601, Commissary of Edinburgh. [NAS]

GRAHAM, JOHN, at the Overmilne, parish of Moffat, 1620. [NAS.CS7/335/265]

GRAHAM, ROBERT, a mason burgess of Dumfries, testament, 1591, Commissary of Edinburgh. [NAS]

GRAHAM, ROBERT, a merchant in Dumfries, father of William Graham, 1679. [NAS.AC7/5]

GRAHAM, ROBERT, bailie and merchant burgess of Dumfries, and spouse Jean Douglas, were granted land in the parish of Kirkpatrick, 1653. [RGS.X.111]

GRAHAM, SAMUEL, from Annandale, a Covenanter banished to the American Plantations in 1685. [RPCS.XI.126/143/145]

GRAHAM, WILLIAM, in Roberthill, parish of Dryfesdale, 1620. [NAS.CS7/335/294]

GRAHAM, WILLIAM, a merchant in Dumfries, 1679. [NAS.AC7/5]

GRAHAM, WILLIAM, a Covenanter killed by government troops in 1682. [Crossmichael gravestone]

GRAY, JOHN, a vagabond and robber in Annandale, to be caught and transported to the American Plantations, 1671. [RPCS.III.428]

GREGAN, THOMAS, in Drumb, testament, 1625, Commissary of Dumfries. [NAS]

GREIG, ROBERT, in Kilquhannudy, testament, 1678, Commissary of Dumfries. [NAS]

GREIR, GILBERT, in Cluben, parish of Balmaghie, 1619. [NAS.CS7/335/63]

GREIR, JAMES, in Kirkandrews, his wife Janet McCulloch, testament, 1606, Commissary of Edinburgh. [NAS]

GRIER, JOHN, from Bigmark, Kirkcudbright, a Covenanter banished to the American Plantations in 1684. [RPCS.X.257]

GRIER, THOMAS, from Cormilligan, Closeburn, Dumfries-shire, a Covenanter banished to the American Plantations in 1684. [RPCS.X.587]

GRIER, Sir WILLIAM, of Lag, 1621. [NAS.E71.10.5]

GREIR, WILLIAM, a merchant in Dumfries, 1622. [NAS.E71.10.5]

GRIERSON, JOHN, formerly in Nether Keir, Dumfries-shire, settled in County Monaghan, by 1639. [CLC#223]

GRIERSON, JOHN, of Keremanoch, parish of Kells, spouse Janet McClellan, testament, 1590, Commissary of Edinburgh. [NAS]

GRIERSON, JOHN, a Covenanter who was killed in 1684. [Dalry gravestone]

GRIERSON, LANCELOT, of Dalstornith, relict Jean Thomas, was granted Mackie in the parish of Torqueir, 1653. [RGS.X.112]

GRIERSON, ROBERT, a Covenanter who was killed by government troops at Ingleston in the parish of Glencairn in 1685. [Balmaclellan gravestone]

GRINDLAY, JOHN, in Roumes, testament, 1659, Commissary of Dumfries. [NAS]

GRINLAW, ADAM, in New Abbey, testament, 1688, Commissary of Dumfries. [NAS]

GUNZEOUN, CHARLES, in Heymayins, parish of Caerlaverock, 1619. [NAS.CS7/335/109]

GUNZEOUN, SYMEON, in Kirkblane, parish of Caerlaverock, 1619. [NAS.CS7/335/109]

HAICHIL, WILLIAM, in Ragaquhat, parish of Dryfesdale, 1620. [NAS.CS7/335/294]

HAINING, ALEXANDER, a cordiner, spouse Katherine Bryce, testament, 1679, Commissary of Dumfries. [NAS]

HAINING, JOHN, in Dinduff, testament, 1627, Commissary of Dumfries. [NAS]

HAIR, GEORGE, a burgess of Annan, testament, 1684, Commissary of Dumfries. [NAS]

HAIR, PATRICK, in Farding, testament, 1659, Commissary of Dumfries. [NAS]

HAIRSTANES, CUTHBERT, in Over Penfillen, parish of Keir testament, 1643, Commissary of Dumfries. [NAS]

HAIRSTANES, JOHN, a merchant burgess in Dumfries, 1621. [NAS.E71.10.5]; heir to his brother Michael Hairstanes of Craigs, 1629. [NAS.Retours, Dumfries#139]

HAIRSTANES, JOHN, in Knockshinnoch, parish of Irongray, an alleged adulterer who fled to Ireland in 1693. [NAS.CH2.1284.2/175]

HAIRSTANES, MATTHEW, of Craigs, 1616. [CLC#1758]

HAISTIE, ROBERT, in Drumeruill testament, 1624, Commissary of Dumfries. [NAS]

HALIDAY, ALEXANDER, in Kilgoun, parish of Anwoth, spouse Janet Gordon, testament, Commissary of Edinburgh, 1600. [NAS]

HALIDAY, ARCHIE, in Tourmuir, parish of Dryfesdale, 1620. [NAS.CS7/335/294]

HALIDAY, DAVID, in Tourmuir, parish of Dryfesdale, 1620. [NAS.CS7/335/294]

HALIDAY, JOHN, son of Fergus Haliday in Lochdouhannis, a witness in 1611. [CLC#1620]

HALIDAY, JOHN, in Tourmuir, parish of Dryfesdale, 1620. [NAS.CS7/335/294]

HALIDAY, JOHN, in Datonhook, parish of Dryfesdale, 1620. [NAS.CS7/335/294]

HALIDAY, SAMUEL, a minister from Ireland, in Dumfries-shire, 1689. [NAS.CH2.1.84.2/40-151]

HALIDAY, THOMAS, a merchant in Dumfries, 1621. [NAS.E71.10.5]

HALIDAY, THOMAS, in Ruttonside, parish of Moffat, 1620. [NAS.CS7/335/265]

HALIDAY, WILLIAM, in Raecleuch, parish of Moffat, 1620. [NAS.CS7/335/265]

HALTHORNE, HARRY, of Meikle Hereis, spouse Agnes Crawford, testament, 1600, Commissary of Edinburgh. [NAS]

HAMILTON, EDWARD, Customs controller at Dumfries, 1613-1613-1621. [NAS.E74.1.4; E74.2.4,7; E71.10.5,7]

HAMILTON, JAMES, minister in Dalry, testament, 1596, Commissary of Edinburgh. [NAS]

HAMILTON, JOHN, born in Sorbie, Wigtownshire, during 1651, eldest son of Reverend Archibald Hamilton, graduated MA from Edinburgh University in 1668, minister at Ballee from 1673 to 1685, in Comber from 1685 to 1689, died 17 October 1702. [FI.65]

HANNA, JOHN, master of the Blessing of Kirkcudbright, 1680, and the Janet of Kirkcudbright, 1682. [NAS.E72.6.5/7]

HANNA, WILLIAM, a Covenanter in Dumfries Tolbooth, transported to East New Jersey in 1685. [RPCS.XI.94/154]

HANNAY, GILBERT, a merchant in Darnestraw, testament, 1594, Commissary of Edinburgh. [NAS]

HANNAY, HUGH, in Grennan, parish of Glenluce, spouse Helen Kennedy, testament, 1599, Commissary of Edinburgh. [NAS]

HANNAY, JOHN, in the parish of Balmaghie, 1619. [NAS.CS7/335/63]

HANNAY, SAMUEL, from Kirkmabreck, Kirkcudbrightshire, a Covenanter who was transported to Barbados in 1679, shipwrecked. [RBM]

HANNAY, WILLIAM, a servant to Patrick Hannay in Wigtownshire, accused of armed assault, fled to Ireland in September 1630. [RPCS.IV.94]

HARKNESS, ALEXANDER, in Lockerbie, parish of Dryfesdale, 1620. [NAS.CS7/335/294]

HARKNESS, DAVID, in Tourmuir, parish of Dryfesdale, 1620. [NAS.CS7/335/294]

HARKNESS, JAMES, in Redhall, testament, 1687, Commissary of Dumfries. [NAS]

HARKNESS, JOHN, a servant in Mitchellslacks, Dumfries-shire, a Covenanter in Dumfries Tolbooth, banished to the American Plantations in 1684. [RPCS.X.309/561/572/587]

HARKNESS, THOMAS, in Lockerbie, parish of Dryfesdale, 1620. [NAS.CS7/335/294]

HARRON, JOHN, in Kirkbryde, parish of Keir, testament, 1680, Commissary of Dumfries. [NAS]

HARVIE, JOHN, a probationer minister at New Abbey, Dumfries-shire, who was called to Ireland in 1689. [NAS.CH2.1284.2/50-251]

HASILHOPE, ROBERT, in Carseada, parish of Lochrutton, 1620. [NAS.CS7.335.311]

HAUGH, JOHN, in Meikle Dalton, testament, 1685, Commissary of Dumfries. [NAS]

HAYNING, WILLIAM, a merchant in Dumfries, 1621. [NAS.E71.10.5]

HEINAN, WILLIAM, in Glenhowen, parish of Caerlaverock, 1619. [NAS.CS7/335/109]

HENDERSON, ANDREW, in Tourmuir, parish of Dryfesdale, 1620. [NAS.CS7/335/294]

HENDERSON, ANDREW, in Thorniewhat, testament, 1657, Commissary of Dumfries. [NAS]

HENDERSON, GAVIN, from Hetland Hill, parish of Mouswald, Dumfriesshire, a merchant traveller in Ireland around 1652. [Mouswald KSR]

HENDERSON, JAMES, in Kirkconnell, 1616. [CLC#4#1758]

HENDERSON, LAURIE, in Mantuarig, parish of Dryfesdale, 1620. [NAS.CS7/335/294]

HENDERSON, ROBERT, a resident of Lochmaben, 1642. [LCC#45]

HENDERSON, THOMSON, minister at Graitney, testaments, 1687, 1688, Commissary of Dumfries. [NAS]

HENDERSON, WILLIAM, in Pottscleuch, parish of Drydesdale, 1620. [NAS.CS7/335/294]

HENDERSON, WILLIAM, in Tourmuir, parish of Dryfesdale, 1620. [NAS.CS7/335/294]

HENDRY, GEORGE, in New Abbey, testament, 1674, Commissary of Dumfries. [NAS]

HENDRY, JAMES, in Over Mossop, parish of Moffat, 1620. [NAS.CS7/335/265]

HENDRY, MICHAEL, spouse Helen Austin, testament, 1659, Commissary of Dumfries. [NAS]

HENNELL, ANDREW, in Datonhook, parish of Dryfesdale, 1620. [NAS.CS7/335/294]

HENRY, MICHAEL, in Counhaith, parish of Caerlaverock, 1619. [NAS.CS7/335/109]

HENRYSON, WILLIAM, in Garkerrow, parish of Kirkcowan, testament, 1593, Commissary of Edinburgh. [NAS]

HERBERTSON, ISOBEL, in Killoside, testament, 1629, Commissary of Dumfries. [NAS]

HERBERTSON, JOHN, a servant of the Earl of Nithsdale, testament, 1680, Commissary of Dumfries. [NAS]

HERON, GILBERT, in Killeill, parish of Penningham, testament, 1590, Commissary of Edinburgh. [NAS]

HERON, HERBERT, in Glencaple, parish of Caerlaverock, 1619. [NAS.CS7/335/109]

HERRIES, BARTILMO, of Over Hessilfield, spouse Janet McMath, testament, 1591, Commissary of Edinburgh. [NAS]

HERRIES, EDWARD, in Little Milton, testament, 1595, Commissary of Edinburgh. [NAS]

HERRIES, EDWARD, in Overbarfell, parish of Lochrutton, 1620. [NAS.CS7/335]

HERRIES, JAMES, a merchant in Dumfries, testament, 1681, Commissary of Dumfries. [NAS]

HERRIES, JOHN, master of the Mayflower of Orr, 1690. [NAS.E72.6.18]

HERRIES, JOHN, in County Antrim, son of John Herries of Little Culloch, Dumfries-shire, sasine, 1693. [NAS.RS22.2.95]

HERRIES, ROBERT, in Greenmill, parish of Caerlaverock, 1619. [NAS.CS7/335/109]

HERRIES, ROBERT, in Lawstoun, parish of Lochrutton, 1620. [NAS.CS7/335/311]

HERRIES, WILLIAM, in Corswada, parish of Lochrutton, 1620. [NAS.CS7/335]

HERRIES, WILLIAM, in Meikle Bogrig, parish of Lochrutton, 1620. [NAS.CS7/335]

HERVIE, JOHN, from Ireland, minister of New Abbey, Dumfries-shire, from 1691 to 1695, then settled in Glen Dermot, Ireland. [F.2.294]

HEUCHAN, MATTHEW, a burgess of Kirkcudbright, testament, 1593, Commissary of Edinburgh. [NAS]

HIDDLESTONE, THOMAS, in Pundland, testament, 1688, Commissary of Dumfries. [NAS]

HILL, GEORGE, a merchant in Dumfries, 1622. [NAS.E71.10.5]

HILL, JOHN, master of the Margaret of Dumfries in 1689, and of the Bonadventure of Dumfries, in 1690. [NAS.E72.6.13/18]

HILLO, JOHN, in Hillotown, his wife Beatrix McGill, testament, 1607, Commissary of Edinburgh. [NAS]

HISLOP, ABRAHAM, in Heymayins, parish of Caerlaverock, 1619. [NAS.CS7/335/109]

HISLOP, JANET, in Sherington, parish of Caerlaverock, 1619. [NAS.CS7/ 335/109]

HISLOP, JOHN, in Bourlands, parish of Caerlaverock, 1619. [NAS.CS7/ 335/109]

HISLOP, ROBERT, a burgess of Dumfries, testament, 1599, Commissary of Edinburgh. [NAS]

HISLOP, ROBERT, in Carswada, parish of Lochrutton, 1620. [NAS.CS7/ 335]

HISLOP, WILLIAM, in Sherington, parish of Caerlaverock, 1619. [NAS.CS7/ 335/109]

HODDAM, JOHN, in Burnside, testament, 1693, Commissary of Dumfries. [NAS]

HOGG, THOMAS, minister at Kirkbean, testament, 1627, Commissary of Dumfries. [NAS]

HOOD, UMPHRA, minister at Torthorwald, testament, 1657, Commissary of Dumfries. [NAS]

HOOK, JAMES, in Ferding, spouse Bessie Black, testament, 1629, Commissary of Edinburgh. [NAS]

HOOPS, JOHN, in Straichanne, testament, 1684, Commissary of Dumfries. [NAS]

HOPE, EDWARD, in Huttonhill, parish of Dryfesdale, 1620. [NAS.CS7/335/ 294]

HOPE, GEORGE, in Auchenslark, parish of Dryfesdale, 1620. [NAS.CS7/ 335/294]

HOPE, JOHN, in Mantuarig, parish of Dryfesdale, 1620. [NAS.CS7/335/ 294]

HOPE, ROBERT, a tailor in Sandyhills, testament, 1684, Commissary of Dumfries. [NAS]

HORNE, ARCHIE, in Datonhook, parish of Dryfesdale, 1620. [NAS.CS7/335/294]

HORNE, DAVID, in Datonhook, parish of Dryfesdale, 1620. [NAS.CS7/335/294]

HORNE, JAMES, in Keltonhook, parish of Dryfesdale, 1620. [NAS.CS7/335/294]

HORSBURGH, ROBERT, a merchant in Dumfries, 1621. [NAS.E71.10.5]

HOSTANE, JOHN, in Newland, parish of Lochrutton, 1620. [NAS.CS7/335]

HOUSOUN, THOMAS, a merchant in Dumfries, 1622. [NAS.E71.10.5]

HOUSTON, JAMES, from Balmaghie, Kirkcudbrightshire, a Covenanter who was transported to Barbados in 1679, shipwrecked. [RBM]

HOUSTON, WILLIAM, a merchant burgess of Whithorn, settled as a merchant in Newcastle, Delaware, died 1707, probate 1711, Newcastle. [DSA.Misc.1/78]

HUME, PATRICK, arrived in Dumfries during 1690 from Ireland. [NAS.CH2.537.15.1/48]

HUNTER, JOHN, in Auchenbreck, parish of Tynron, spouse Bessie Douglas, testament, 1598, Commissary of Edinburgh. [NAS]

HUNTER, JOHN, in Kirkconnell, parish of Tynron, testament, 1599, Commissary of Edinburgh. [NAS]

HUNTER, JOHN, a minister who fled from Ireland in 1689, and settled in Kirkmichael, Wigtownshire. [RPCS.XVI.336]

HUTCHISON, JOHN, a merchant in Kirkcudbright, 1641. [NAS.E73.9.7]

HUTCHISON, ROBERT, in Hill, testament, 1658, Commissary of Dumfries. [NAS]

HUTTON, HERBERT, in Nether Carse, testament, 1681, Commissary of Dumfries. [NAS]

HUTTON, JOHN, in Counhaith, parish of Caerlaverock, 1619. [NAS.CS7/335/109]

HYND, JAMES, a merchant in Dumfries, deed, 1697. [NAS.RD4.81.1102]

INGLIS, JOHN, burgess of Kirkcudbright, spouse Janet Gledstanes, testament, 1595, Commissary of Edinburgh. [NAS]

INGLIS, JOHN, in Bargatoun, parish of Balmaghie, 1619. [NAS.CS7/335/63]

INGLIS, MARY, arrived in Dumfries during 1690 from Ireland. [NAS.CH2.537.15.1/40]

IRELAND, JAMES, born 1652, died 6 May 1724, his wife Margaret Anderson died 17 June (1724?) aged 63. [Balmaclellan gravestone]

IRELAND, JOHN, in Canzell, testament, 1596, Commissary of Edinburgh. [NAS]

IRELAND, WILLIAM, in Dincow, testament, 1657, Commissary of Dumfries. [NAS]

IRVING, ANDREW, in Lockerbie, parish of Dryfesdale, 1620. [NAS.CS7/335/294]

IRVING, DAVID, in Auchinsark, parish of Dryfesdale, 1620. [NAS.CS7/335/294]

IRVING, DAVID, a merchant in Dumfries, 1622. [NAS.E71.10.5]

IRVING, GEORGE, a merchant burgess of Dumfries, testament, 1638, Commissary of Dumfries. [NAS]

IRVING, EDWARD, a merchant in Dumfries, 1622. [NAS.E71.10.5]

IRVING, EDWARD, a resident of Lochmaben, 1642. [LCC#45]

IRVING, FRANCIS, a merchant in Dumfries, trading with Flanders, 1622. [NAS.E71.10.5]

IRVING, GEORGE, a merchant in Dumfries, 1622. [NAS.E71.10.5]

IRVING, HERBERT, a merchant burgess of Dumfries, spouse Isobel Carlisle, testament, 1661, Commissary of Dumfries. [NAS]

IRVING, JOHN, in Bengall, parish of Dryfesdale, 1620. [NAS.CS7/335/294]

IRVING, JOHN, the elder and the younger, in Auchenslark, parish of Dryfesdale, 1620. [NAS.CS7/335/294]

IRVING, JOHN, a merchant in Dumfries, trading with Flanders, 1622. [NAS.E71.10.5]

IRVING, JOHN, a bailie of Dumfries, deed, 1699. [NAS.RD3.90.627]

IRVING, JOHN, a merchant in Dumfries, deed, 1699. [NAS.RD2.83.404]

IRVING, THOMAS, in Auchelslark, parish of Dryfesdale, 1620. [NAS.CS7/335/294]

IRVING, THOMAS, born in Ecclefechan, Dumfries-shire, around 1667, fought overseas in the service of King William, settled in Bardarroch, died in October 1711. . [Anwoth gravestone]

IRVING, THOMAS, a merchant in Dumfries, deed, 1699. [NAS.RD3.90.627]

IRVING, WILLIAM, in Lockerbie, parish of Dryfesdale, 1620. [NAS.CS7/335/294]

IRVING, WILLIAM, in Skar, parish of Dryfesdale, 1620. [NAS.CS7/335/294]

IRVING, WILLIAM, a merchant in Dumfries, trading with Flanders, 1622. [NAS.E71.10.5]

IRVING, WILLIAM, of Bonshaw, deed, 1699. [NAS.RD2.83.330]

JACKSON. JAMES, at Wamphrey Gate, testament, 1674, Commissary of Dumfries. [NAS]

JACKSON, WILLIAM, in Milbie, testament, 1684, Commissary of Dumfries. [NAS]

JAFFRAY, THOMAS, in Blackshaw, parish of Caerlaverock, 1619. [NAS.CS7/335/109]

JAMIESON, JANET, and her son Robert Dickson, in Sherington, parish of Caerlaverock, 1619. [NAS.CS7/335/109]

JAMIESON, JOHN, in Cleuchfutts, testament, 1658, Commissary of Dumfries. [NAS]

JARDINE, ALEXANDER, heir to his father John Jardine of Applegirth, in the Stewartry of Annandale, 1643. [NAS.Retours, Dumfries#174]

JARDINE, GAVIN, in Counhaith, parish of Caerlaverock, 1619. [NAS.CS7/335/109]

JARDINE, JAMES, in Lockerbie, testament, 1685, Commissary of Dumfries. [NAS]

JARDINE, WILLIAM, in Langholm, parish of Dryfesdale, 1620. [NAS.CS7/335/294]

JARDINE, WILLIAM, a merchant from Dumfries, a member of the Scots Charitable Society of Boston in 1684. [NEHGS/SCS]

JOHNSTON, ADAM, in Riddings, parish of Moffat, 1620. [NAS.CS7/335/265]

JOHNSTON, ADAM, in Huttonhill, parish of Dryfesdale, 1620. [NAS.CS7/335/294]

JOHNSTON, ADAM, a resident of Lochmaben, 1642. [LCC#45]

JOHNSTON, ADAM, the elder, a resident of Lochmaben, 1642. [LCC#45]

JOHNSTON, AGNES, in Roundstounfoot, parish of Moffat, 1620. [NAS.CS7/335/265]

JOHNSTON, ALEXANDER, the younger of Elsheills, provost of Lochmaben, 1684. [LCC#179]

JOHNSTON, ANDREW, in Catlins, parish of Dryfesdale, 1620. [NAS.CS7/335/294]

JOHNSTON, ANDREW, in Auldwells, parish of Dryfesdale, 1620. [NAS.CS7/335/294]

JOHNSTON, ANDREW, in Roberthill, parish of Dryfesdale, 1620. [NAS.CS7/335/294]

JOHNSTON, ANDREW, a merchant in Dumfries, 1621. [NAS.E71.10.5]

JOHNSTON, ARCHIE, in Overbyres, parish of Dryfesdale, 1620. [NAS.CS7/335/294]

JOHNSTON, BESSIE, in Nether Landwoodend, parish of Moffat, 1620. [NAS.CS7/335/265]

JOHNSTON, BESSIE, in Lockerbie, parish of Dryfesdale, 1620. [NAS.CS7/335/294]

JOHNSTON, CHRISTIAN, in Fuldoris, parish of Dryfesdale, 1620. [NAS.CS7/335/294]

JOHNSTON, CUTHBERT, in the Hallis, parish of Dryfesdale, 1620. [NAS.CS7/335/294]

JOHNSTON, DAVID, in Boghead, parish of Dryfesdale, 1620. [NAS.CS7/335/294]

JOHNSTON, DAVID, in Annan, testament, 1691, Commissary of Dumfries. [NAS]

JOHNSTON, EDWARD, in the parish of Moffat, 1620. [NAS.CS7/335/265]

JOHNSTON, FRANCIS, arrived in Dumfries during 1690 from Ireland. [NAS.CH2.537.15.1/29]

JOHNSTON, GEORGE, of Quaas, parish of Dryfesdale, 1620. [NAS.CS7/335/294]

JOHNSTON, GEORGE, in Nulbank, parish of Dryfesdale, 1620. [NAS.CS7/335/294]

JOHNSTON, GILBERT, in Hendlehead, parish of Moffat, 1620. [NAS.CS7/335/265]

JOHNSTON, GILBERT, in Strone, parish of Dryfesdale, 1620. [NAS.CS7/335/294]

JOHNSTON, GILES, in Auchenslark, parish of Dryfesdale, 1620. [NAS.CS7/335/294]

JOHNSTON, HARBERT, in Dryisholme, parish of Dryfesdale, 1620. [NAS.CS7/335/294]

JOHNSTON, HERCULES, in Lockerbie, parish of Dryfesdale, 1620. [NAS.CS7/335/294]

JOHNSTON, HEW, in Corhead, parish of Moffat, 1620. [NAS.CS7/335/265]

JOHNSTON, JAMES, in Dryisholme, parish of Dryfesdale, 1620. [NAS.CS7/335/294]

JOHNSTON, JAMES, of Lochhouse, parish of Moffat, 1620. [NAS.CS7/335/265]

JOHNSTON, JAMES, in Hendlehead, parish of Moffat, 1620. [NAS.CS7/335/265]

JOHNSTON, JAMES, of Lochhouse, parish of Moffat, 1620. [NAS.CS7/335/265]

JOHNSTON, JAMES, in Ruttonside, parish of Moffat, 1620. [NAS.CS7/335/265]

JOHNSTON, JAMES, in the parish of Dryfesdale, 1620. [NAS.CS7/335/294]

JOHNSTON, JAMES, of Luss, parish of Dryfesdale, 1620. [NAS.CS7/335/294]

JOHNSTON, JAMES, in Broomhill, a resident of Lochmaben, 1642. [LCC#45]

JOHNSTON, JAMES, in Langholm, spouse Janet Brown, testament, 1682, Commissary of Dumfries. [NAS]

JOHNSTON, JANET, of Vicarland, parish of Moffat, 1620. [NAS.CS7/335/265]

JOHNSTON, JOHN, parish of Dryfesdale, 1620. [NAS.CS7/335/294]

JOHNSTON, JOHN, in Nulbamk, parish of Dryfesdale, 1620. [NAS.CS7/335/294]

JOHNSTON, JOHN, in Cleuchhead, parish of Dryfesdale, 1620. [NAS.CS7/335/294]

JOHNSTON, JOHN, in Woodhead, parish of Moffat, 1620. [NAS.CS7/335/265]

JOHNSTON, JOHN, in the parish of Moffat, 1620. [NAS.CS7/335/265]

JOHNSTON, JOHN, in Auldwells, parish of Dryfesdale, 1620. [NAS.CS7/335/294]

JOHNSTON, JOHN, in Mantuarig, parish of Dryfesdale, 1620. [NAS.CS7/335/294]

JOHNSTON, JOHN, in Torwood, parish of Dryfesdale, 1620. [NAS.CS7/335/294]

JOHNSTON, JOHN, in Hairhope, parish of Moffat, 1620. [NAS.CS7/335/265]

JOHNSTON, JOHN, in Catlins, parish of Dryfesdale, 1620. [NAS.CS7/335/294]

JOHNSTON, JOHN, of the Hill, parish of Dryfesdale, 1620. [NAS.CS7/335/294]

JOHNSTON, JOHN, a merchant in Dumfries, 1631. [NAS.AC7/2/386]

JOHNSTON, JOHN, of Shaw, a resident of Lochmaben, 1642. [LCC#45]

JOHNSTONE, JOHN, from Drysdale, Dumfries-shire, a merchant in Carrickfergus, Ireland, sasine,1654; deed, 1666; who died before November 1679, father of William. [NAS.RS22.6.2; RD4.16.498; Retours, Dumfries]

JOHNSTON, JOHN, spouse Janet Bowie, testament, 1679, Commissary of Dumfries. [NAS]

JOHNSTON, JOHN, a miller and councillor of Lochmaben, 1684. [LCC#179]

JOHNSTON, or BRUMELL, JOHN, a councillor of Lochmaben, 1684. [LCC#179]

JOHNSTON, JOHN, of Selclothe, relict Anna Brown, testament, 1687, Commissary of Dumfries. [NAS]

JOHNSTON, JOHN, and family, arrived in Dumfries during 1690 from Ireland. [NAS.CH2.537.15.1/27]

JOHNSTON, MARY, arrived in Dumfries during 1690 from Ireland. [NAS.CH2.537.15.1/35]

JOHNSTON, MUNGO, in Greenhill, parish of Moffat, 1620. [NAS.CS7/335/265]

JOHNSTON, NICOLL, in Wellwood, parish of Drydesdale, 1620. [NAS.CS7/335/294]

JOHNSTONE, ROBERT, parson of Lochmaben, residing in Carnesalloch, parish of Kirkmahoe, testament, 1592, Commissary of Edinburgh. [NAS]

JOHNSTON, ROBERT, in Meikleholmside, parish of Moffat, 1620. [NAS.CS7/335/265]

JOHNSTON, ROBERT, in the parish of Moffat, 1620. [NAS.CS7/335/265]

JOHNSTON, ROBERT, in Revox, parish of Moffat, 1620. [NAS.CS7/335/265]

JOHNSTONE, ROBERT, provost of Dumfries, 1695. [NAS.AC13/5/20]

JOHNSTON, ROBERT, in Fuldoris, parish of Dryfesdale, 1620. [NAS.CS7/335/294]

JOHNSTON, ROWLAND, in Nether Landwoodend, parish of Moffat, 1620. [NAS.CS7/335/265]

JOHNSTONE, SIMON, a merchant burgess of Dumfries, testament, 1590, Commissary of Edinburgh. [NAS]

JOHNSTON, SIMON, in Woodhead, parish of Moffat, 1620. [NAS.CS7/335/265]

JOHNSTON, THOMAS, of Ersbank, parish of Moffat, 1620. [NAS.CS7/335/265]

JOHNSTON, THOMAS, in Hairhope, parish of Moffat, 1620. [NAS.CS7/335/265]

JOHNSTON, THOMAS, in Revox in the parish of Moffat, 1620. [NAS.CS7/335/265]

JOHNSTON, THOMAS, in the parish of Moffat, 1620. [NAS.CS7/335/265]

JOHNSTON, THOMAS, in Broomhouse, parish of Dryfesdale, 1620. [NAS.CS7/335/294]

JOHNSTON, THOMAS, a bailie of Lochmaben, 1684. [LCC#179]

JOHNSTONE, THOMAS, master of the Providence of Dumfries, 1689. [NAS.E72.6.13]

JOHNSTON, WALTER, in Greenhill, parish of Moffat, 1620. [NAS.CS7/335/265]

JOHNSTON, WILLIAM, in Fuldoris, parish of Dryfesdale, 1620. [NAS.CS7/335/294]

JOHNSTON, WILLIAM, in Broomhouse, parish of Dryfesdale, 1620. [NAS.CS7/335/294]

JOHNSTON, WILLIAM, in Boghead, parish of Dryfesdale, 1620. [NAS.CS7/335/294]

JOHNSTON, WILLIAM, in Halldykes, parish of Dryfesdale, 1620. [NAS.CS7/335/294]

JOHNSTON, WILLIAM, in Lockerbie, parish of Dryfesdale, 1620. [NAS.CS7/335/294]

JOHNSTON, WILLIAM, in the parish of Moffat, 1620. [NAS.CS7/335/265]

JOHNSTON, WILLIAM, in Cowanhouse, parish of Dryfesdale, 1620. [NAS.CS7/335/294]

JOHNSTON, WILLIAM, in Ruttonside, parish of Moffat, 1620. [NAS.CS7/335/265]

JOHNSTON, WILLIAM, a resident of Lochmaben, 1642. [LCC#45]

JOHNSTON, WILLIAM, heir to his father John Johnston a merchant in Carrickfergus, Ireland, re lands in the parish of Drysdale, 1679. [NAS.Retours, Dumfries#301]

JOHNSTON, WILLIAM, formerly in Netherly Park, Kirkcudbrightshire, then in Bellewillwill, County Down, 1699. [Kirkcudbright Sheriff Court Deeds#3356]

JOURRELL, JOHN, spouse Agnes Anderson, testament, 1657, Commissary of Dumfries. [NAS]

KAE, CHRISTOPHER, a workman in Dumfries, testament, 1625, Commissary of Dumfries. [NAS]

KAILLIE, DAVID, in Dalskairth, testament, 1657, Commissary of Dumfries. [NAS]

KARKO, JAMES, in Adingham, testament, 1624, Commissary of Dumfries. [NAS]

KAY, THOMAS, in Chlistbrae, parish of Dryfesdale, 1620. [NAS.CS7/335/294]

KEITH, WILLIAM, a burgess of Wigtown, spouse Katherine McDowall, testament, 1600, Commissary of Edinburgh. [NAS]

KELLOCK, JOHN, a cordiner in Sanquhar, testament, 1659, Commissary of Dumfries. [NAS]

KELTON, JOHN, in Bordland, testament, 1685, Commissary of Dumfries. [NAS]

KELTON, MARION, in Datonhook, parish of Dryfesdale, 1620. [NAS.CS7/ 335/294]

KENNAN, JOHN, in Ilestepps, testament, 1628, Commissary of Dumfries. [NAS]

KENNAN, ROBERT, in Laghall, testament, 1658, Commissary of Dumfries. [NAS]

KENNEDY, ALEXANDER, of Craigoich, 1654. [RGS.X.588]

KENNEDY, ARCHIBALD, in Barneill, spouse Annabel Cunningham, testament, 1595, Commissary of Edinburgh. [NAS]

KENNEDY, FERGUS, heir to his father Fergus Kennedy in Bellilochan, Ireland, former provost of Stranraer, 1664. [NAS.Retours.Wigtown#145]

KENNEDY, GEORGE, a merchant in Dumfries, 1622. [NAS.E71.10.5]

KENNEDY, HEW, in Dryisholme, parish of Dryfesdale, 1620. [NAS.CS7/ 335/294]

KENNEDY, JAMES, in Beckton, parish of Dryfesdale, 1620. [NAS.CS7/ 335/294]

KENNEDY, JAMES, of Barnkirk in the parish of Machrihochell, Ireland, heir to his father Archibald Kennedy of Barnkirk, re lands in the parish of Penningham, 1680. [NAS.Retours.Wigtown#161]

KENNEDY, JOHN, in Glendrissock, parish of Kells, testament, 1591, Commissary of Edinburgh. [NAS]

KENNEDY, JOHN, and Janet Ireland, in Craigs, parish of Balmaghie, 1619. [NAS.CS7/335/63]

KENNEDY, JOHN, from Closeburn, Dumfries-shire, a Covenanter who was transported to Barbados in 1679, shipwrecked. [RBM]

KENNEDY, MARTIN, in Bannekirk, testament, 1595, Commissary of Edinburgh. [NAS]

KENNEDY, MUNGO, in Auchenslark, parish of Dryfesdale, 1620. [NAS.CS7/335/294]

KENNEDY, THOMAS, in Kerebrine, parish of Kirkinner, testament, 1596, Commissary of Edinburgh. [NAS]

KENNEDY, WILLIAM, in Tourmuir, parish of Dryfesdale, 1620. [NAS.CS7/335/294]

KENNEDY, WILLIAM, a resident of Lochmaben, 1642. [LCC#45]

KENT, JOHN, the elder, testament, 1658, Commissary of Dumfries. [NAS]

KERR, ALEXANDER, in Mollochford, parish of Penpont, testament, 1638, Commissary of Dumfries. [NAS]

KERR, JOHN, in Dumbreck, testament, 1657, Commissary of Dumfries. [NAS]

KID, JANET, daughter of John Kid, in Glenhonan, testament, 1676, Commissary of Dumfries. [NAS]

KILPATRICK, HUGH, born in Dumfries-shire, a minister in Lurgan, Ireland, from 1685 to 1688, then in Ballimoney from 1693, died 1 April 1712. [FI#71][NAS.GD18.4019]

KINCAID, JOHN, a Covenanter in Wigtown and Dumfries Tolbooths, transported to East New Jersey in 1685. [RPCS.XI.154]

KINCAID, JOHN, a merchant in Glen Luce, deed, 1699. [NAS.RD2.82.323]

KIPPERT, JOHN, in Corswada, parish of Lochrutton, 1620. [NAS.CS7/335]

KIRK, GILBERT, in Kilbein, testament, 1659, Commissary of Dumfries. [NAS]

KIRK, JOHN, in Boigland, parish of Dalgarnock, testament, 1640, Commissary of Dumfries. [NAS]

KIRKO, ADAM, in Glenisland, parish of Dunscore, testament, 1592, Commissary of Edinburgh. [NAS]

KIRKO, JOHN, heir to his father John Kirko portioner of Glengaber, 1692. [NAS.Retours, Dumfries#335]

KIRKPATRICK, JOHN, a merchant burgess of Dumfries, testament, 1600, Commissary of Edinburgh. [NAS]

KIRKPATRICK, JOHN, in Ryes, spouse Margaret Beck, testament, 1676, Commissary of Dumfries. [NAS]

KIRKPATRICK, ROBERT, of Branko, parish of Holywood, testament, 1590, Commissary of Edinburgh. [NAS]

KIRKPATRICK, ROBERT, in Swadyland alias Langrigsland, parish of Caerlaverock, 1619. [NAS.CS7/335/109]

KIRKPATRICK, ROGER, in Dursdow, testament, 1597, Commissary of Edinburgh. [NAS]

KIRKPATRICK, THOMAS, in Dumfries, spouse Janet Anderson, testament, 1641, Commissary of Dumfries. [NAS]

KNEISCHE, EDWARD, in Bardristan, testament, 1609, Commissary of Edinburgh. [NAS]

KYD, PAUL, in Counhaith, parish of Caerlaverock, 1619. [NAS.CS7/335/109]

LACHLISON, JOHN, of Burnside, parish of Dunscore, testament, 1683, Commissary of Dumfries. [NAS]

LAIDLAW, JAMES, in Todholls, parish of Sanquhar, testament, 1692, Commissary of Dumfries. [NAS]

LAIDLAY, JAMES, in Burrenclech, testament, 1681, Commissary of Dumfries. [NAS]

LAING, JOHN, in Blackgarroch, testament, 1657, Commissary of Dumfries. [NAS]

LATTIMER, RICHARD, in Lochmaben, testament, 1656, Commissary of Dumfries. [NAS]

LAUDER, ANDREW, an apothecary in Ireland, son of Reverend Andrew Lauder in Whithorn, deed, 1671. [NAS.RD3.27.263]

LAWRENCE, WILLIAM, a resident of Lochmaben, 1642. [LCC#45]

LAWRIE, ALEXANDER, a labourer from Dumfries, emigrated via Bristol to Virginia in 1658. [Bristol Record Office#04220]

LAWRIE, JOHN, schoolmaster of Kirkcudbright, deed, 1673. [NAS.RD4.4.67]

LAWRIE, JOHN, of Maxwellton, testament, 1685, Commissary of Dumfries. [NAS]

LAWRIE, WILLIAM, a merchant burgess of Dumfries, testament, 1630, Commissary of Dumfries. [NAS]

LAWSON, JOHN, a merchant burgess of Dumfries, spouse Jean Barton, testament, 1675, Commissary of Dumfries. [NAS]

LAWSON, WILLIAM, a tailor in Dumfries, testament, 1682, Commissary of Dumfries. [NAS]

LEITCH, DAVID, a vagabond and robber in Annandale, to be caught and transported to the American Plantations, 1671. [RPCS.III.428]

LENNOX, ANDREW, of Pluntoun, parish of Kirkandrews, his wife Janet Lennox, testament, 1598, Commissary of Edinburgh. [NAS]

LEWARS, JOHN, in Barr, spouse Janet Aiton, testaments, 1656, 1657, Commissary of Dumfries. [NAS]

LEWARS, JOHN, a merchant burgess of Dumfries, testament, 1679, Commissary of Dumfries. [NAS]

LIDDELL, JOHN, in Boytathe, testament, 1684, Commissary of Dumfries. [NAS]

LIGHTON, RONALD, in Auchenflour, parish of Kirkcudbright, testament, 1597, Commissary of Edinburgh. [NAS]

LINDSAY, ADAM, in Hightae, testament, 1657, Commissary of Dumfries. [NAS]

LINDSAY, JOHN, of Main, born 1623, died 26 February 1665, his wife Isobella McLellan, born 1617, died 26 January 1695. [Southwick gravestone]

LINDSAY, ROGER, in the Mains, relict Janet Maxwell, testament, 1600, Commissary of Edinburgh. [NAS]

LINTON, WILLIAM, burgess of Kirkcudbright, spouse Bessie Gledstanes, testament, 1598, Commissary of Edinburgh. [NAS]

LISTSTER, GEORGE, in Woodhead, testament, 1659, Commissary of Dumfries. [NAS]

LITSTER, WALTER, in Annan, testament, 1639, Commissary of Dumfries. [NAS]

LITTLE, MATTHEW, in Bombie, testament, 1679, Commissary of Dumfries. [NAS]

LITTLE, THOMAS, a merchant in Dumfries, 1621. [NAS.E71.10.5]

LITTLE, WILLIAM, in Burnfoot of Eskdale, spouse Janet Armstrong, testament, 1684, Commissary of Dumfries. [NAS]

LIVINGSTON, ALEXANDER, in Cullenoch, parish of Balmaghie, 1619. [NAS.CS7/335/63]

LIVINGSTON, GEORGE, in Cullenoch, parish of Balmaghie, 1619. [NAS.CS7/335/63]

LIVINGSTONE, WILLIAM, minister at Sanquhar, testament, 1625, Commissary of Dumfries. [NAS]

LOCKARBIE, JOHN, in Mantuarig, parish of Dryfesdale, 1620. [NAS.CS7/335/294]

LOCKARBIE, MATHEW, in Auchinslark, parish of Dryfesdale, 1620. [NAS.CS7/335/294]

LOCKARBIE, WILLIAM, in Mantuarig, parish of Dryfesdale, 1620. [NAS.CS7/335/294]

LOCKHART, THOMAS, a merchant burgess of Dumfries, testament, 1685, Commissary of Dumfries. [NAS]

LOGAN, JOHN, and spouse Mary Linton, in Dumfries, testament, 1685, Commissary of Dumfries. [NAS]

LORIMER, JOHN, parish of Lochrutton, 1620. [NAS.CS7.335.311]

LOTTIMER, RICHARD, a resident of Lochmaben, 1642. [LCC#45]

LOWRIE, JOHN, in Woodfoot, parish of Lochrutton, 1620. [NAS.CS7/335]

LOWRIE, STEVEN, a merchant in Dumfries, trading with Flanders, 1622. [NAS.E71.10.5]

LOWRIE, THOMAS, in Whiteyard, parish of Lochrutton, 1620. [NAS.CS7/335]

LYN, FERGUS, a merchant in Dumfries, 1621. [NAS.E71.10.5]

LYN, FERGUS, of Large, 1636. [RGS.X.588]

LYN, JOHN, in Kerezeild, parish of Kirkmahoe, spouse Katherine Robson, testament, 1592, Commissary of Edinburgh. [NAS]

MCADAM, CHRISTIAN, daughter of the late George McAdam in Langford, parish of Kells, testament, 1595, Commissary of Edinburgh. [NAS]

MCADAM, CHRISTIAN, Lady Cardynes, born 1595, died 16 June 1626. [Anwoth gravestone]

MCBIRNIE, BESSIE, in Over Crae, parish of Balmaghie, 1619. [NAS.CS7/335/63]

MCBIRNIE, FRANCES, in Uliock, parish of Balmaghie, 1619. [NAS.CS7/335/63]

MCBIRNIE, JANET, in Drumglas, parish of Balmaghie, 1619. [NAS.CS7/335/63]

MCBIRNIE, WILLIAM, in Beandknock, parish of Balmaghie, 1619. [NAS.CS7/335/63]

MCBRAIR, CHRISTIAN, in Nether Crae, parish of Balmaghie, 1619. [NAS.CS7/335/63]

MCBRAIR, DAVID, of Newark, testament, 1680, Commissary of Dumfries. [NAS]

MCBRAIR, GAVIN, of Bourlands, parish of Caerlaverock, 1619. [NAS.CS7/335/109]

MCBRAIR, JOHN, in Counhaith, parish of Caerlaverock, 1619. [NAS.CS7/335/109]

MCBRAIR, ROBERT, of Craig, parish of Kirkmabreck, a messenger, deed, 1697. [NAS.RD4.81.907]

MCBRAIR, ROBERT, a messenger in Dumfries, deed, 1697. [NAS.RD4.80.433]

MCBRAIR, THOMAS, a merchant burgess of Dumfries, testament, 1642, Commissary of Dumfries. [NAS]

MCBRATNEY, JOHN, from Galloway, a Covenanter who was transported to Barbados in 1679, shipwrecked. [RBM]

MCBRYDE, JOHN, heir to his father Alexander McBryde a merchant burgess of Stranraer, 1667. [NAS.Retours.Wigtown#148]

MCBRYDE, MICHAEL, and spouse Mallie McNeillie, in Craigbirrenach, parish of Glenluce, testament, 1592, Commissary of Edinburgh. [NAS]

MCBURNE, EDWARD, in Woodend of the Bankend, parish of Caerlaverock, 1619. [NAS.CS7/335/109]

MCBURNE, ROBERT, in Holmends, parish of Caerlaverock, 1619. [NAS.CS7/335/109]

MCBURNE, ROBERT, in Kirkblane, parish of Caerlaverock, 1619. [NAS.CS7/335/109]

MCBURNIE, JOHN, a shoemaker in Dumfries, testament, 1689, Commissary of Dumfries. [NAS]

MCBURNIE, MARTIN, miller at Redkirk Mill, testament, 1673, Commissary of Dumfries. [NAS]

MCCADEIN, ANDREW, of Walterhead, testament, 1590, Commissary of Edinburgh. [NAS]

MCCAIG, HELEN, testament, 1659, Commissary of Dumfries. [NAS]

MCCAIG, NICOLL, in Sandrem, testament, 1674, Commissary of Dumfries. [NAS]

MCCALL, GEORGE, in Dalpedder, parish of Kirkbride, testament, 1590, Commissary of Edinburgh. [NAS]

MCCALL, JOHN, in Nether Dalpedden, parish of Kirkbride, spouse Esther Barbour, testament, 1638, Commissary of Dumfries. [NAS]

MCCALL, JOHN, in Castlemains of Sanquhar, spouse Janet Blacklock, testament, 1638, Commissary of Dumfries. [NAS]

MCCALLUM, JOHN, in Arnecraig, parish of Crossmichael, testament, 1599, Commissary of Edinburgh. [NAS]

MCCANCHIE, ALEXANDER, in Crochmore, testament, 1658, Commissary of Dumfries. [NAS]

MCCARMICK, Sir JAMES, in Corrichrie, parish of Kirkmaiden, spouse Agnes MacMaster, testament, 1595, Commissary of Edinburgh. [NAS]

MCCARTNEY, GEORGE, in Camdudzell, his wife Blanch Henderson, testament, 1601, Commissary of Edinburgh. [NAS]

MCCARTNEY, JAMES, in Finenish, parish of Balmaghie, 1619. [NAS.CS7/335/63]

MCCARTNEY, JOHN, from Kirkcudbright, a Covenanter who was transported to Barbados in 1679, shipwrecked. [RBM]

MCCARTNEY, WALTER, in Glentove, parish of Balmaghie, 1619. [NAS.CS7/335/63]

MCCARTNEY, WILLIAM, in Chappellerne, parish of Crossmichael, testament, 1598, Commissary of Edinburgh. [NAS]

MCCHURRIE, JOHN, in Ward of Kirkgunzeon, testament, 1657, Commissary of Dumfries. [NAS]

MCCHYNE, THOMAS, in Blackwood, testament, 1657, Commissary of Dumfries. [NAS]

MCCLAUCHRIE, ROGER, in Beoch, parish of Kirkpatrick- Irongray, testament, 1639, Commissary of Dumfries. [NAS]

MCCLEISS, WILLIAM, a burgess of Kirkcudbright, spouse Christine Martin, testament, 1595, Commissary of Edinburgh. [NAS]

MCCLELLAN, ALEXANDER, in Gattuay, testament, 1594, Commissary of Edinburgh. [NAS]

MCCLELLAN, JOHN, in Almernes, parish of Buittle, testament, 1597, Commissary of Edinburgh. [NAS]

MCCLELLAN, JOHN, in Overlaw, parish of Rerrick, spouse Agnes Ramsay, testament, 1600, Commissary of Edinburgh. [NAS]

MCCLELLAN, JOHN, in Townhead of Frenchland, parish of Moffat, 1620. [NAS.CS7/335/265]

MCCLELLAN, THOMAS, of Balmangand, his wife Janet McClelland, testament, 1605, Commissary of Edinburgh. [NAS]

MCCLELLAN, WILLIAM, of Balmangan, testament, 1607, Commissary of Edinburgh. [NAS]

MCCLELLAND, ANDREW, a Covenanter, transported to East New Jersey in 1685. [RPCS.XI.155]

MCCLELLAND, JOHN, born in Kirkcudbright during 1609, son of Michael McClelland, educated at Glasgow University from 1626 to 1629, graduated MA, a schoolmaster in County Down, attempted to emigrate to New England on the Eagle Wing in 1636, returned to Scotland, died 1650, husband of (1) Marion, daughter of Bartholemew Fleming in Edinburgh, (2) Isabel McClelland. [PHS]

MCCLELLAND, Sir ROBERT, of Bombie, and Isobel, eldest daughter of Sir Hew Montgomery of Newton, marriage contract, 1612; 1617. [NAS.RH15/91.12, 59]

MCCLELLAND, ROBERT, a Covenanter, transported to East New Jersey in 1685. [RPCS.XI.155/292]

MCCLELLAND, THOMAS, of Nunton, parish of Kirkchrist, testament, 1593, Commissary of Edinburgh. [NAS]

MCCLELLAND, THOMAS, of Bomby, testament, 1598, Commissary of Edinburgh. [NAS]

MCCLELLAND, WILLIAM, in Barnegaithing, parish of Kirkandrews, testament, 1592, Commissary of Edinburgh. [NAS]

MCCLELLAND, WILLIAM, of Gregorie, testament, 1598, Commissary of Edinburgh. [NAS]

MCCLELLAND, WILLIAM, of Orchardton, a freeholder in Ulster, 1620s. [NAS.RH15.91.33]

MCCLEN, GILBERT, a merchant in Dumfries, 1621. [NAS.E71.10.5]

MCCLERIE, UCHREID, in the parish of Kirkmaiden, testament, 1595, Commissary of Edinburgh. [NAS]

MCCLINGAN, ALEXANDER, fled to Ireland between 1679 and 1689. [Penningham KSR, 19.2.1711]

MCCLUN, RODGER, in Cluben, parish of Balmaghie, 1619. [NAS.CS7/335/63]

MCCLURE, SIMON, in Edgarton, parish of Balmaghie, 1619. [NAS.CS7/335/63]

MCCLYMONT, JOHN, in Correoch, testament, 1593, Commissary of Edinburgh. [NAS]

MCCONACHIE, JOHN, in Cruiffok, parish of Girthon, testament, 1594, Commissary of Edinburgh. [NAS]

MCCONCHIE, ROBERT, in Ireland, son of Alexander Moore, a merchant burgess of Wigtown, 1659. [Kirkcudbright Sheriff Court Deeds #43]

MCCONNELL, GILBERT, miller in Culmalzow, parish of Kirkinner, testament, 1599, Commissary of Edinburgh. [NAS]

MCCOSKRES, JOHN, born 1674, resident of Lagan Mulloch, died 1718, his wife Mary Carson, born 1666, died in February 1737. [Anwoth gravestone]

MCCOWAN, JOHN, in Greenmill, parish of Caerlaverock, 1619. [NAS.CS7/335/109]

MCCOWTRIE, JOHN, son of the late John McCowtrie in Gablabrigs, parish of Morton, testament, 1690, Commissary of Dumfries. [NAS]

MCCRACKEN, JOHN, in Gillespik, parish of Glenluce, testament, 1599, Commissary of Edinburgh. [NAS]

MCCRERIE, ELIZABETH, a widow in Dumfries, testament, 1656, Commissary of Dumfries. [NAS]

MCCRONE, THOMAS, in Maibie, testament, 1657, Commissary of Dumfries. [NAS]

MCCRONE, WILLIAM, in Drummilling, testament, 1674, Commissary of Dumfries. [NAS]

MCCUBBIN, JAMES, in Are, parish of Balmaghie, 1619. [NAS.CS7/335/63]

MCCUBBIN, JOHN, in Sanquhar, testament, 1641, Commissary of Dumfries. [NAS]

MCCUEAN, WALTER, a Covenanter, transported to the American Plantations in 1685. [RPCS.XI.154]

MCCULLOCH, ALEXANDER, of Ardwell, was granted Logan etc in Wigtownshire, 1657. [RGS.X.588]

MCCULLOCH, DAVID, of Druchtag, heir to his father John McCulloch of Druchtag, Wigtown, 1600. [NAS.S/H]

MCCULLOCH, JAMES, of Drummorrell, Wigtownshire, was enrolled as an Undertaker for the Plantation of Ulster with a grant of 2000 acres in 1609. [RPCS.VIII.329]; was granted lands in County Donegal, 1611. [Cal.SP.Ire.1611/384]

MCCULLOCH, WILLIAM, of Ardwell, testament, 1603, Commissary of Edinburgh. [NAS]

MCCUNE, JOHN, in Craigneston, testament, 1627, Commissary of Dumfries. [NAS]

MCCUNE, NINIAN, in Cleuchhead of Sundaywell, testament, 1628, Commissary of Dumfries. [NAS]

MCDOUGAL, ROBERT, in Muircroft, testament, 1684, Commissary of Dumfries. [NAS]

MCDOWALL, AGNES, spouse of Roger McNaught in the Braid of Ireland, deed, 1622; in County Antrim, sasine, 1688. [NAS.RD4.6.389; RS22.4.374]

MCDOWALL, ANDREW, of Killaisor, 1657. [RGS.X.588]

MCDOWALL, FERGUS, member of the Scots Charitable Society of Boston in 1684. [NEHGS/SCS]

MCDOWALL, GILBERT, in Barlockhart, parish of Glenluce, testament, 1599, Commissary of Edinburgh. [NAS]

MCDOWALL, HUGH, of Elrig, parish of Kirkmaiden, testament, 1599, Commissary of Edinburgh. [NAS]

MCDOWALL, HUGH, of Kinking, 1636. [RGS.X.588]

MCDOWALL, JAMES, in Balmacraill, relict Margaret MacNeish, testament, 1592, Commissary of Edinburgh. [NAS]

MCDOWALL, JOHN, a wright burgess of Kirkcudbright, testament, 1595, Commissary of Edinburgh. [NAS]

MCDOWALL, JOHN, of French, parish of Stoneykirk, testament, 1592, Commissary of Edinburgh. [NAS]

MCDOWALL, JOHN, of Knockincrosne, testament, 1594, Commissary of Edinburgh. [NAS]

MCDOWALL, JOHN, heir to his father Uchtred McDowell of Garthland, Wigtown, 1600. [NAS.S/H]

MCDOWALL, Sir JOHN, of Garthland, 1636. [RGS.X.588]

MCDOWALL, QUENTIN, in Galdernoch, parish of Saulseat, testament, 1593; spouse Isabel McMaster, testament, 1598, Commissary of Edinburgh. [NAS]

MCDOWALL, ROBERT, heir to his father Patrick McDowall of Logan, 1699. [NAS.Retours.Wigtown#191]

MCDOWALL, UCHREID, in Kildonnan, testament, 1599, Commissary of Edinburgh. [NAS]

MCDOWALL UCHRID, of Freuch, 1657. [RGS.X.588]

MACDUFF, JOHN, died 1681, his wife Marion Hendry, died 1687. [Colvend gravestone]

MCEWAN, JOHN, in Craig, testament, 1601, Commissary of Edinburgh. [NAS]

MCFAZEAN, JOHN, portioner of Killilego, testament, 1674, Commissary of Dumfries. [NAS]

MCFADZEAN, WILLIAM, the elder, in Berdwell, parish of Dunscore, testament, 1592, Commissary of Edinburgh. [NAS]

MCGEACHEN, JOHN, the younger, of Dalquhat, testament, 1625, Commissary of Dumfries. [NAS]

MCGEOCH, ALAN, in Drumwhirrie, spouse Katherine McMillan, testament, 1597, Commissary of Edinburgh. [NAS]

MCGEORGE, WILLIAM, clerk to the Fleshers of Dumfries, 1679. [DAC]

MCGIE, ALEXANDER, of Balmaghie, deed, 1699. [NAS.RD4.84.1202]

MCGIE, JOHN, from Kirkcudbright, a Covenanter who was transported to Barbados in 1679, shipwrecked. [RBM]

MCGIE, JOHN, a merchant in Kirkcudbright, the younger, deed, 1699. [NAS.RD2.82.783]

MCGIE, MICHAEL, in Kirkgunzeon, deed, 1699. [NAS.RD4.85.1137]

MCGIE, NINIAN, in Clacharie, parish of Kirkinner, spouse Janet Gibson, testament, 1596, Commissary of Edinburgh. [NAS]

MCGIE, WILLIAM, of Balmaghie, deed, 1699. [NAS.RD4.84.1200]

MCGILL, JOHN, in Meikle Knox, his wife Beatrix Carsan, testament, 1608, Commissary of Edinburgh. [NAS]

MCGILL, JOHN, a merchant burgess of Edinburgh, was granted lands in Kirkconnell etc, 1658. [RGS.X.668]

MCGIRRE, ROBERT, in Dalbeattie, testament, 1658, Commissary of Dumfries. [NAS]

MCGOUN, KATHERINE, in Dornald, parish of Balmaghie, 1619. [NAS.CS7/335/63]

MCGOUN, PATRICK, in Cotton Netherlaw, parish of Rerrick, spouse Marion Hornwell, testament, 1600, Commissary of Edinburgh. [NAS]

MCGOURLIE, JOHN, of Garverie, testament, 1597, Commissary of Edinburgh. [NAS]

MCGOWAN, JAMES, in Drumlane, parish of Balmaghie, 1619. [NAS.CS7/ 335/63]

MCGOWAN, JAMES, a merchant in Dumfries, 1622. [NAS.E71.10.5]

MCGOWAN, JOHN, in Theifgrang, parish of Balmaghie, 1619. [NAS.CS7/ 335/63]

MCGOWAN, JOHN, in Lochside Croft, parish of Lochrutton, 1620. [NAS.CS7/335]

MCGUB, JANET, in Markland of Allanton, testament, 1657, Commissary of Dumfries. [NAS]

MCGUFFOCK, ARCHIBALD, in Uliock, parish of Balmaghie, 1619. [NAS.CS7/335/63]

MCGUFFOCK, GEORGE, in Craigs, parish of Balmaghie, 1619. [NAS.CS7/ 335/63]

MCGUFFOCK, JAMES, in Drumlane, parish of Balmaghie, 1619. [NAS.CS7/335/63]

MCHARG, JOHN, with his wife and three children, arrived in Dumfries during 1690 from Ireland. [NAS.CH2.537.15.1/36]

MCILDOWNIE, ROBERT, minister at Cummertrees, testament, 1624, Commissary of Dumfries. [NAS]

MCILDUFF, JOHN, a merchant in Girthon, testament, 1594, Commissary of Edinburgh. [NAS]

MCILDUFF, ROBERT, in Bank of Hillis, parish of Lochrutton, 1620. [NAS.CS7/335]

MCILNAY, JOHN, in Uroche, parish of Balmaghie, 1619. [NAS.CS7/335/63]

MCILNAY, WILLIAM, in Uroche, parish of Balmaghie, 1619. [NAS.CS7/335/63]

MCILNO, ANDREW, in Lochhead, parish of Kells, testament, 1594, Commissary of Edinburgh. [NAS]

MCILLNO, JAMES, in Crofts, his wife Isobel McGarmorie, testament, 1604, Commissary of Edinburgh. [NAS]

MCILLNO, JAMES, in Crofts, his wife Agnes Graham, testament, 1606, Commissary of Edinburgh. [NAS]

MCILPHERSON, JAMES, a vagabond and robber in Annandale, to be caught and transported to the American Plantations, 1671. [RPCS.III.428]

MCILROSSE, JOHN, in Polmemady, testament, 1674, Commissary of Dumfries. [NAS]

MCILWAYLL, DAVID, a merchant burgess of Dumfries, testament, 1661, Commissary of Dumfries. [NAS]

MCILWENE, JOHN, at Kilmafadzean, parish of Glenluce, testament, 1591, Commissary of Edinburgh. [NAS]

MCJORE, WILLIAM, schoolmaster of Dumfries, spouse Katherine Copland, 1660s. [NAS.RD2.12.571; RD2.18.600]

MCKAIG, JOHN, arrived in Dumfries during 1690 from Ireland. [NAS.CH2.537.15.1/35]

MCKEAND, THOMAS, in Spittal, testament, 1598, Commissary of Edinburgh. [NAS]

MCKENZIE, JOHN, in Dryburgh, testament, 1593, Commissary of Edinburgh, his widow Helen Murray, testament, 1598, Commissary of Edinburgh. [NAS]

MCKENZIE, PATRICK, a burgess of Stranraer, and co-owner of the bark Providence of Stranraer, 1675. [NAS.AC7/9]

MCKERVAIL, DAVID, from Glencairn, Dumfries-shire, a Covenanter who was transported to Barbados in 1679, shipwrecked. [RBM]

MCKESSOCK, HENRY, a burgess of Kirkcudbright, testament, 1598, Commissary of Edinburgh. [NAS]

MCKEWEN, JOHN, in Belliebocht, Londonderry, sasine, 1645. [NAS.RS22.4.129]

MCKEVAT, PATRICK, in Mains of Duchray, parish of Balmaghie, 1619. [NAS.CS7/335/63]

MCKEVAT, ROBERT, in Mains of Duchray, parish of Balmaghie, 1619. [NAS.CS7/335/63]

MACKIE, ALEXANDER, at the Kirk of Crossmichael, testament, 1608, Commissary of Edinburgh. [NAS]

MCKIE, ALLAN, in Lybirk, parish of Kirkinner, spouse Christine Mitche....,, testament, 1599, Commissary of Edinburgh. [NAS]

MCKIE, EDWARD, of Rotchell, Kirkcudbrightshire, formerly in Kilstalpen, Ireland, 1643. [NAS.RS22.5.65]

MACKIE, HUGH, master of the Adventure of Dumfries, 1688, and of the Margaret of Dumfries, 1689. [NAS.E72.6.11/15]

MCKIE, JOHN, in Glenvogue, parish of Penninghame, testament, 1591, Commissary of Edinburgh. [NAS]

MCKIE, JOHN, in Glenturpok, parish of Mochrum, spouse Marion McKie, testament, 1592, Commissary of Edinburgh. [NAS]

MCKIE, JOHN, in Stronba, parish of Minnigaff, testament, 1597, Commissary of Edinburgh. [NAS]

MCKIE, JOHN, a burgess of Wigtown, testament, 1598, Commissary of Edinburgh. [NAS]

MCKIE, PATRICK, of Larg, parish of Minnigaff, spouse Janet McDowall, testament, 1594, Commissary of Edinburgh. [NAS]

MCKIE, Sir PATRICK, of Larg, Minnigaff, Wigtownshire, an Undertaker in County Donegal, 1611. [Cal.SP.Ire.1611/384]

MCKIE, THOMAS, a merchant burgess of Belfast, Ireland, heir to his father Patrick McKie of Cairn, Wigtownshire,1688. [NAS.Retours. Wigtown#172]

MCKIE, WILLIAM, in Torririe, spouse Margaret Brown, testament, 1686, Commissary of Dumfries. [NAS]

MCKILL, ALEXANDER, in Crogo, parish of Balmaclellan, his wife Margaret McMichael, testament, 1599, Commissary of Edinburgh. [NAS]

MCKILL, FINLAY, in Dirgoull, parish of Minnigaff, widow Bessie Heron, testament, 1599, Commissary of Edinburgh. [NAS]

MCKINNELL, WILLIAM, Deacon Convenor of the Trades of Dumfries, testament, 1674, Commissary of Dumfries. [NAS]

MCKINNEY, DAVID, in Capitanton, testament, 1658, Commissary of Dumfries. [NAS]

MCKINSHE, GILBERT, a cordiner at the Bridgend of Dumfries, testament, 1628, Commissary of Dumfries. [NAS]

MCKITTRICK, WILLIAM, a bailie of Dumfries, testament, 1678, Commissary of Dumfries. [NAS]

MCKLRIN (?), JOHN, died May 1702. [Southwick gravestone]

MCKNAIGHT, JOHN, of Kirkland of Balmaghie, Kirkcudbrightshire, and Adam Vance in Donnachadee, County Down, a bond, 1682. [Kirkcudbright Sheriff Court Deeds #1063]

MCKNAIGHT, JOHN, of Cullfield, bound for Ireland in 1694. [Kirkcudbright Sheriff Court Deed #2666]

MCKOUN, MARGARET, born 1663, died 2 February 1734. [Anwoth gravestone]

MCLEAN, GILBERT, a merchant burgess of Dumfries, testament, 1625, Commissary of Dumfries. [NAS]

MCCLELLAN, HERBERT, of Gregorie, applied for a grant of 2000 acres in Ireland during 1609. [RPCS.VIII.329]

MCLELLAN, MARGARET, a Covenanter in Dumfries Tolbooth, transported to East New Jersey in 1685. [RPCS.XI.154/291/292]

MCLELLAN, MATTHEW, son of John MacLellan of Orcougule, Galloway, emigrated via Bristol to Barbados in 1655. [Bristol Record Office]

MCLELLAN, Sir ROBERT, of Bomby, Galloway, granted denization and land in Donegal, 1610. [IPR]

MCLELLAN, ROBERT, of Barmagachan, deed, 1696. [NAS.RD2.79.762]

MCLURG, JOHN, in Farrochba, parish of Minnigaff, testament, 1600, Commissary of Edinburgh. [NAS]

MCMARTIN, JOHN, in Capenoch, testament, 1643, Commissary of Dumfries. [NAS]

MCMATH, JAMES, of Dalpeddar, testament, 1624, Commissary of Dumfries. [NAS]

MCMATH, JOHN, a tailor in Castle Gilmour, parish of Kirkbride, testament, 1590, spouse Janet McCanerick, testament, 1593, Commissary of Edinburgh. [NAS]

MCMAYTH, JOHN, heir to his father Roger McMayth, re lands in the barony of Sanquhar, 1601. [NAS.Retours, Dumfries#12]

MCMICHAEL, ROGER, from Dalry, Galloway, a Covenanter who was transported to Jamaica in 1685. [RPCS.XI.316]

MCMILLAN, ALEXANDER, from Galloway, a Covenanter who was transported to Barbados in 1685. [RPCS.XI.386]

MCMILLAN, GEORGE, in Holme of Dalcallachan, parish of Kells, testament, 1591, Commissary of Edinburgh. [NAS]

MCMILLAN, JOHN, in Lamaquhen, Galloway, testament, 1592, Commissary of Edinburgh. [NAS]

MCMILLAN, JOHN, of Brocloch, died 30 November 1674, possibly his wife Betrag (Beatrix?) Aird, died 1666. [Carsphairn gravestone]

MCMILLAN, JOHN, born 1645, died 1715, his wife Margaret Akin, born 1647, died 1724. [Balmaclellan gravestone]

MCMILLAN, JOHN, born 1663, minister in Balmaghie, died 26 July 1700, his wife Catherine Williamson, died 31 August 1700. [Balmaghie gravestone]

MCMILLAN, JOHN, son of Reverend John McMillan in Balmaclellan, testament, 1693, Commissary of Edinburgh. [NAS]

MCMILLAN, JOHN, of Brokloch, born 1664, died 28 February 1725. [Carsphain gravestone]

MCMILLAN, JOHN, born during 1669 in Barncauchlaw, parish of Minnigaff, minister at Balmaghie from 1701-1727, co-founder of the Reformed Presbyterian Church in 1743, died at Broomhill, Bothwell, on 1 December 1753. [Balmaghie gravestone]

MCMILLAN, THOMAS, in Marscalloch, parish of Dalry, testament, 1592, Commissary of Edinburgh. [NAS]

MCMILLAN, THOMAS, a merchant in Dumfries, trading with Flanders, 1622. [NAS.E71.10.5]

MCMILLAN, WILLIAM, born 1689, buried 22 July 1703. [Carsphairn gravestone]

MCMORRAN, EDWARD, in Lochrutton Gait, parish of Lochrutton, 1620. [NAS.CS7/335]

MCMORRAN, JOHN, in Nether Croft, parish of Lochrutton, 1620. [NAS.CS7/335]

MCMORRAN, THOMAS, in Barlochan, parish of Buittle, testament, 1599, Commissary of Edinburgh. [NAS]

MCMORRIE, JAMES, a merchant burgess of Dumfries, testament, 1675, Commissary of Dumfries. [NAS]

MCMUNE, GEORGE, in Redcastle, testament, 1685, Commissary of Dumfries. [NAS]

MCMURDIE, ROBERT, heir to his father John McMurdie in Dunscore, 1602. [NAS.Retours, Dumfries#15]

MCMURDIE, ..., daughter of Robert McMurdie in Kelligo Craig, Dumfries, and wife of John Johnston in Drumboe, Ireland, sasine, 1681. [NAS.RS22.3.157-9]

MCNAB, JOHN, in Bridgend, testament, 1673, Commissary of Dumfries. [NAS]

MCNAE, JOHN, born 1640, a resident of Gatehouse of Fleet, parish of Girthon, died there in August 1723. [Anwoth gravestone]

MCNAUCHT, DAVID, in Meikle Mochrum, parish of Parton, testament, 1594, Commissary of Edinburgh. [NAS]

MCNAUGHT, GILBERT, in Blackcraig, testament, 1604, Commissary of Edinburgh. [NAS]

MCNAUGHT, GILBERT, in Meikleholmside, parish of Moffat, 1620. [NAS.CS7/335/265]

MCNAUGHT, JAMES, a merchant in New Galloway, deed, 1696. [NAS.RD2.80.291]

MCNAUGHT, JOHN, of Kilquhannadie, parish of Kirkpatrick-Durham, testament, 1599, Commissary of Edinburgh. [NAS]

MCNAUGHT, ROGER, in County Antrim, dead by 1688, sasine. [NAS.RS22.4.374]

MCNAULD, MICHAEL, in Torris, testament, 1595, Commissary of Edinburgh. [NAS]

MCNAULD, THOMAS, in Little Torris, testament, 1595, Commissary of Edinburgh. [NAS]

MCNEILLIE, JOHN, in Barnevannock, parish of Kirkcudbright, spouse Margaret McCalmont, testament, 1592, Commissary of Edinburgh. [NAS]

MCNEISH, JOHN, a merchant in Kerrymanoch, testament, 1594, Commissary of Edinburgh. [NAS]

MCNEVIN, GILBERT, in Corhousemackie, parish of Wigtown, testament, 1598, Commissary of Edinburgh. [NAS]

MCNEVIN, WILLIAM, in Blackmark, parish of Wigtown, spouse Margaret McCall, testament, 1600, Commissary of Edinburgh. [NAS]

MCQUEEN, JOHN, in Cluben, parish of Balmaghie, 1619. [NAS.CS7/335/63]

MCQUEEN, ROBERT, a Covenanter from Nithsdale, transported to East New Jersey in 1685. [RPCS.XI.154]

MCQUHA, WILLIAM, in Glentove, parish of Balmaghie, 1619. [NAS.CS7/335/63]

MCQUHAN, ANDREW, from Kirkcudbright, a Covenanter who was transported to Barbados in 1679, shipwrecked. [RBM]

MCQUHAN, THOMAS, from Kirkcudbright, a Covenanter who was transported to Barbados in 1679, shipwrecked. [RBM]

MCQUHARIE, THOMAS, in the parish of Caerlaverock, 1619. [NAS.CS7/335/109]

MCQUHONE, GILBERT, a merchant in Dumfries, trading with Flanders, 1622. [NAS.E71.10.5]

MCQUHRIK, JOHN, in Bariokart, parish of Glenluce, testament, 1600, Commissary of Edinburgh. [NAS]

MCQUIRRIE, or MCWHIRRIE, GEORGE, in Drumboy, parish of Kells, widow Janet Dougalston, testament, 1598, Commissary of Edinburgh. [NAS]

MCTAGGART, JAMES, in Gathgill, testament, 1606, Commissary of Edinburgh. [NAS]

MCTAGGART, JAMES, born 1670, resident of Archland, died 1716, father of Patrick. [Anwoth gravestone]

MCTAGGART, JOHN, from Penninghame, Wigtownshire, a Covenanter who was transported to Barbados in 1679, shipwrecked. [RBM]

MCTAGGART, MICHAEL, and his family, fled to Ireland between 1679 and 1689. [Penningham KSR, 19.2.1711]

MCTAGGART, THOMAS, in Carndurrie, parish of Minnigaff, testament, 1595, Commissary of Edinburgh. [NAS]

MCTHIR, BRADIE, a merchant in Lagbaus, testament, 1596, Commissary of Edinburgh. [NAS]

MCTURK, DAVID, testament, 1657, Commissary of Dumfries. [NAS]

MCVITIE, ARCHIBALD, in Stubholm, testament, 1679, Commissary of Dumfries. [NAS]

MCWHAE, ROBERT, a Covenanter who was killed in Kirkandrews in 1685.[Kirkandrews gravestone]

MCWHARRIE, JAMES, son to the late Thomas McWharrie, a merchant in Dumfries, testament, 1688, Commissary of Dumfries. [NAS]

MCWHIRR, JOHN, in Larglawche, testament, 1624, Commissary of Dumfries. [NAS]

MCWILLIAM, GILBERT, in Drumscott, parish of Mochrum, testament, 1598, Commissary of Edinburgh. [NAS]

MCWILLIAM, WILLIAM, in Greenhead, Mains of Caerlaverock, testament, 1659, Commissary of Dumfries. [NAS]

MABAN, JOHN, in Conhaith, parish of Caerlaverock, testament, 1639, Commissary of Dumfries. [NAS]

MAIN, JAMES, in the parish of Moffat, 1620. [NAS.CS7/335/265]

MAIR, ALEXANDER, minister at Kirkmahoe, testament, 1689, Commissary of Dumfries. [NAS]

MAITLAND, JAMES, in Knockhowghlie, testament, 1690, Commissary of Dumfries. [NAS]

MALCOLM, JOHN, from Dalry, Galloway, a Covenanter who was transported to Barbados in 1679, shipwrecked. [RBM]

MALCOLM, ROBERT, the younger, in Auchinschean, testament, 1596, Commissary of Edinburgh. [NAS]

MALCOLMSON, WILLIAM, in the Dylce, Sanquhar, testament, 1596, Commissary of Edinburgh. [NAS]

MAN, THOMAS, in Corbellie, testament, 1674, Commissary of Dumfries. [NAS]

MARKIE, PATRICK, former provost of Whithorn, 1684. [NAS.AC7/6]

MARSHALL, ANDREW, in Glenwadey, parish of Kirkbean, testament, 1638, Commissary of Dumfries. [NAS]

MARSHALL, JOHN, a burgess of Dumfries, testament, 1626, Commissary of Dumfries. [NAS]

MARTIN, ADAM, a cordiner in the parish of Caerlaverock, 1619. [NAS.CS7/335/109]

MARTIN, ANDREW, in Borg, testament, 1598, Commissary of Edinburgh. [NAS]

MARTIN, JAMES, fled to Ireland between 1679 and 1689. [Penningham KSR, 19.2.1711]

MARTIN, JOHN, a writer in Dumfries, 1611. [CLC#1620]

MARTIN, JOHN, in the parish of Caerlaverock, 1619. [NAS.CS7/335/109]

MARTIN, JOHN, in Clone, parish of Balmaghie, 1619. [NAS.CS7/335/63]

MARTIN, JOHN, in the parish of Moffat, 1620. [NAS.CS7/335/265]

MARTIN, JOHN, Deacon of the Fleshers of Dumfries, 1679. [DAC]

MARTIN, JOHN, from Borgue, Kirkcudbrightshire, a Covenanter who was transported to Barbados in 1679, shipwrecked. [RBM]

MARTIN, JOHN, a messenger in Dumfries, deed, 1699. [NAS.RD2.83.562]

MARTIN, MARGARET, heir to her father John Martin a burgess of Whithorn, 1636. [NAS.Retours. Wigtown#90]

MARTIN, NICOLL, in Heymayins, parish of Caerlaverock, 1619. [NAS.CS7/335/109]

MARTIN, PATRICK, a merchant burgess of Wigtown, testament, 1591, Commissary of Edinburgh. [NAS]

MARTIN, ROBERT, in Lochhouse, parish of Moffat, 1620. [NAS.CS7/335/265]

MARTIN, ROBERT, son of John Martin a flesher, was admitted as a journeyman to the Fleshers Incorporation of Dumfries on 30 September 1659. [DAC]

MARTIN, ROBERT, arrived in Dumfries during 1690 from Ireland. [NAS.CH2.537.15.1/25]

MARTIN, THOMAS, in Erectstane, parish of Moffat, 1620. [NAS.CS7/335/265]

MARTIN, WILLIAM, in Rone, parish of Balmaghie, 1619. [NAS.CS7/335/63]

MARTIN, WILLIAM, in Blackshaw, parish of Caerlaverock, 1619. [NAS.CS7/335/109]

MARTIN, WILLIAM, a merchant in Dumfries, 1622. [NAS.E71.10.5]

MARTIN, WILLIAM, a merchant traveller in England, and spouse Katherine Alexander, testament, 1682, Commissary of Dumfries. [NAS]

MATHESON, JOHN, from Closeburn, Dumfries-shire, a Covenanter, transported to Carolina in 1684. [Edinburgh Tolbooth Records][RPCS.IX.15]

MATHESON, PATRICK, in Overtormolland, parish of Balmaghie, 1619. [NAS.CS7/335/63]

MAXWELL, ALEXANDER, emigrated from Halls, Tynwald, to Ireland before 1690. [NAS.CH2.537.15.2/75-98]

MAXWELL, BARBARA, in Crofts, parish of Lochrutton, 1620. [NAS.CS7/335]

MAXWELL, BARBARA, widow of James Geddes of Barbachill, in Thirdpart, parish of Lochrutton, 1620. [NAS.CS7.335.311]

MAXWELL, CHRISTIAN, in Blackshaw, parish of Caerlaverock, 1619. [NAS.CS7/335/109]

MAXWELL, EDWARD, of Ile, parish of Caerlaverock, 1619. [NAS.CS7/335/109]

MAXWELL, EDWARD, in Carswada, parish of Lochrutton, 1620. [NAS.CS7/335/311]

MAXWELL, HERBERT, of Kirkconnell, son and heir of the late John Maxwell of Kirkconnell, a witness, (brother germane of John and James Maxwell), 1613/1614/1616/1617. [CLC#1690/1702/1755/1758]

MAXWELL, HUGH, in Preston, parish of Kirkbean, spouse Janet Dickson, testament, 1598, Commissary of Edinburgh. [NAS]

MAXWELL, JAMES, brother-germane to Robert, Earl of Nithsdale, 1621. [NAS.E71.10.5]

MAXWELL, JAMES, a merchant in Dumfries, 1622; 1631. [NAS.E71.10.5; AC7/2/386]

MAXWELL, JAMES, clerk to the Fleshers of Dumfries, died 1678. [DAC]

MAXWELL, JAMES, of Kirkconnell, deed, 1699. [NAS.RD3.90.386]

MAXWELL, JANET, wife of John Leighton in County Tyrone, sasine, 1680. [NAS.RS22.3.50]

MAXWELL, JOHN, of Mains of Buittle, testament, 1599, Commissary of Edinburgh. [NAS]

MAXWELL, JOHN, son of Alexander Maxwell of Logan, a witness, 1611. [CLC#1620]

MAXWELL, JOHN, in Bourlands, parish of Caerlaverock, 1619. [NAS.CS7/335/109]

MAXWELL, JOHN, in Conhaith, parish of Caerlaverock, 1619. [NAS.CS7/335/109]

MAXWELL, JOHN, in Bankend, parish of Caerlaverock, 1619. [NAS.CS7/335/109]

MAXWELL, JOHN, in Lochwood of Bourlands, parish of Caerlaverock, 1619. [NAS.CS7/335/109]

MAXWELL, JOHN, in Overbarfell, parish of Lochrutton, 1620. [NAS.CS7/335]

MAXWELL, JOHN, of Dalswinton, 1654. [RGS.X.306]

MAXWELL, NICOL, in Dirnaban, County Tyrone, 1671. [NAS.RS22.1.28]

MAXWELL, ROBERT, in Hemayns, parish of Caerlaverock, 1619. [NAS.CS7/335/109]

MAXWELL, Sir ROBERT, of Orchardton, now resident of Ireland, deed of factory, 1688. [Kirkcudbright Sheriff Court Deeds #1265]

MAXWELL, WILLIAM, late bailie, a resident of Lochmaben, 1642. [LCC#45]

MAXWELL, WILLIAM, the younger, a resident of Lochmaben, 1642. [LCC#45]

MAXWELL, WILLIAM, of Munreth, was granted lands in the parish of Kirkinner, 1658. [RGS.X.643]

MEEK, ROBERT, in Mote, parish of Lochrutton, 1620. [NAS.CS7/335]

MENZIES, JOHN, of Castlehill, parish of Durisdeer, testament, 1642, Commissary of Dumfries. [NAS]

MILLER, AGNES, in Lochfoot, parish of Lochrutton, 1620. [NAS.CS7/335]**MILLER, FLORA,** in Mote, parish of Lochrutton, 1620. [NAS.CS7/335]

MILLER, JOHN, the elder, in Lochfoot, parish of Lochrutton, 1620. [NAS.CS7/335]

MILLER, JOHN, the younger, in Lochfoot, parish of Lochrutton, 1620. [NAS.CS7/335]

MILLER, KATHERINE, in Grange Mylne, parish of Dunscore, testament, 1596, Commissary of Edinburgh. [NAS]

MILLER, ROBERT, elder and younger, in Mote, parish of Lochrutton, 1620. [NAS.CS7/335]

MILLER, WILLIAM, from Glencairn, Nithsdale, a Covenanter who was transported to Barbados in 1679, shipwrecked. [RBM]

MILLIGAN, JOHN, from Glencairn, Nithsdale, a Covenanter who was transported to Barbados in 1679, shipwrecked. [RBM]

MILLIGAN, PETER, his wife Jane Murra died 1693. [Colvend gravestone]

MILLIGAN, THOMAS, from Glencairn, Nithsdale, a Covenanter who was transported to Barbados in 1679, shipwrecked. [RBM]

MILLIGAN, WILLIAM, at the Nether Mylne of Arbigland, spouse Isobel Brown, testament, 1675, Commissary of Dumfries.

MILLIKEN, HOMER, in Dryisholme, parish of Dryfesdale, 1620. [NAS.CS7/335/294]

MIRRIE, THOMAS, a merchant in Dumfries, 1622. [NAS.E71.10.5]

MITCHELL, ALEXANDER, from Kirkcudbright, a freeholder in Ulster, 1620s. [NAS.RH15.91.33]

MITCHELL, ROBERT, a merchant burgess of Dumfries, testament, 1592, Commissary of Edinburgh. [NAS]

MITCHELSON, GILBERT, the elder, in Whiteyard, parish of Lochrutton, 1620. [NAS.CS7/335]

MITCHELSON, PATRICK, in Auchinfrans, parish of Lochrutton, 1620. [NAS.CS7/335/311]

MITCHELSON, RICHARD, in Lawstoun, parish of Lochrutton, 1620. [NAS.CS7/335/311]

MOFFAT, ADAM, in Heddriehauch, parish of Moffat, 1620. [NAS.CS7/335/265]

MOFFAT, JAMES, of Nethermilne, parish of Moffat, 1620. [NAS.CS7/335/265]

MOFFAT, JAMES, a merchant in Dumfries, 1621. [NAS.E71.10.5]

MOFFAT, JOHN, in Townhead of Frenchland, parish of Moffat, 1620. [NAS.CS7/335/265]

MOFFAT, MATTHEW, of Granton, parish of Moffat, 1620. [NAS.CS7/335/265]

MOFFAT, MUNGO, in the parish of Moffat, 1620. [NAS.CS7/335/265]

MOFFAT, ROBERT, in Granton, parish of Moffat, 1620. [NAS.CS7/335/265]

MOFFAT, ROBERT, in Meikleholmside, parish of Moffat, 1620. [NAS.CS7/335/265]

MOFFAT, WILLIAM, in Greenknow, parish of Dryfesdale, 1620. [NAS.CS7/335/294]

MONTGOMERIE, HUGH, of Grangehioh, County Londonderry, brother of George Montgomerie in Kirkcudbright, commission, 1670. [Kirkcudbright Sheriff Court Deeds #937]

MONTGOMERY, KATHERINE, arrived in Dumfries during 1690 from Ireland. [NAS.CH2.537.15.1/27]

MORE, MARION, in Cullindach, died 1612. [Anwoth gravestone]

MORING, JOHN, of Morington, testament, 1642, Commissary of Dumfries. [NAS]

MORRIS, JOHN, in Auchenslark, parish of Dryfesdale, 1620. [NAS.CS7/ 335/294]

MORRISON, EDWARD, of Addingham, parish of Urr, testament, 1600, Commissary of Edinburgh. [NAS]

MORRISON, HUGH, at the Mill of Edingham, testament, 1689, Commissary of Dumfries. [NAS]

MORTON, JOHN, in Keir, testament, 1657, Commissary of Dumfries. [NAS]

MORTON, ROBERT, a webster at the Bridgend of Dumfries, testament, 1657, Commissary of Dumfries. [NAS]

MOSSMAN, MUNGO, a smith in Dalgoner, testament, 1657, Commissary of Dumfries. [NAS]

MUDIE, GILBERT, and his mother Agnes Johnston, in the parish of Moffat, 1620. [NAS.CS7/335/265]

MUDIE, JOHN, in the parish of Moffat, 1620. [NAS.CS7/335/265]

MUIR, ANDREW, born 1660, resident of Upper Rusco, died 1724. [Anwoth gravestone]

MUIR, JAMES, born 1652, resident of Halfmark, Anwoth, died there 1717. [Anwoth gravestone]

MUIRHEAD, DAVID, in Mains of Barnbachill, parish of Lochrutton, 1620. [NAS.CS7/335/311]

MULLIGAN, ANDREW, the elder, and the younger, in Hall of Barquhar, parish of Lochrutton, 1620. [NAS.CS7/335]

MULLIGAN, JAMES, in Hall of Barquhar, parish of Lochrutton, 1620. [NAS.CS7/335]

MULLIGAN, PAUL, in the parish of Balmaghie, 1619. [NAS.CS7/335/63]

MULLIGAN, RICHARD, in Arngannoch, parish of Balmaghie, 1619. [NAS.CS7/335/63]

MULLIGAN, ROBERT, sometime in Lochrutton, a traveller in Ireland, witness, 1683. [Kirkcudbright Sheriff Court Deeds #882]

MULLIGAN, THOMAS, in Auchinfrans, parish of Lochrutton, 1620. [NAS.CS7/335]

MULLIGAN, WILLIAM, in Ruchill Croft, parish of Lochrutton, 1620. [NAS.CS7/335]

MUNCIE, JAMES, a tailor burgess of Dumfries, testament, 1686, Commissary of Dumfries, 1686. [NAS]

MUNDELL, JAMES, miller at Tynwald Mill, testament, 1685, Commissary of Dumfries. [NAS]

MUNDELL, JOHN, from Dumfries, a member of the Scots Charitable Society of Boston in 1694. [NEHGS/SCS]

MURDOCH, ALEXANDER, in Drumglas, parish of Balmaghie, 1619. [NAS.CS7/335/63]

MURDOCH, JANET, in Clachan of Minnigaff, testament, 1598, Commissary of Edinburgh. [NAS]

MURDOCH, JOHN, in Drumglas, parish of Balmaghie, 1619. [NAS.CS7/335/63]

MURDOCH, JOHN, in Little Duchray, parish of Balmaghie, 1619. [NAS.CS7/335/63]

MURDOCH, JOHN, born 1659, minister of Crossmichael, died 1 August 1700, his wife Agnes Colden, born 1659, died 13 May 1732. [Crossmichael gravestone]

MURDOCH, JOHN, from Glencairn, Nithsdale, a Covenanter who was transported to Barbados in 1679, shipwrecked. [RBM]

MURDOCH, PATRICK, in Camloden, parish of Minnigaff, spouse Marie Geddes, testament, 1598, Commissary of Edinburgh. [NAS]

MURDOCH, WILLIAM, born 1635, died 1682, his wife Jean Ker, born 1641, died April 1704. [Dalry gravestone]

MURE, ANDREW, at St John's Chapel, parish of Saulseat, testament, 1593, Commissary of Edinburgh. [NAS]

MURMAN, JAMES, in Townhead of Frenchland, parish of Moffat, 1620. [NAS.CS7/335/265]

MURMAN, ROBERT, in Townhead of Frenchland, parish of Moffat, 1620. [NAS.CS7/335/265]

MURRAY, ALEXANDER, from Penninghame, Wigtownshire, a Covenanter who was transported to Barbados in 1679, shipwrecked. [RBM]

MURRAY, ANDREW, in Hewcleuch, parish of Moffat, 1620. [NAS.CS7/335/265]

MURRAY, GEORGE, of Broughton, Wigtownshire, was enrolled as an Undertaker for the Plantation of Ulster with a grant of 2000 acres in 1609. [RPCS.VIII.317]

MURRAY, GEORGE, the younger, of Murraythwaite, deed, 1697. [NAS.RD4.81.223]

MURRAY, JAMES, the Earl of Annandale, Governor of Donegal, 1641. [CLC#2293]

MURRAY, JAMES, in Inchkeill, Ireland, heir to his father Alexander Murray of Blackcraigs, re lands in the parish of Rerrick, 1670. [NAS.Retours, Kirkcudbright#319]

MURRAY, JAMES, in Killibegs, County Donegal, 1698, son of Richard Murray of Broughton, Wigtownshire. [CLC#2968]

MURRAY, JOHN, of Dundrennan, 1613. [CLC#1690]

MURRAY, JOHN, of Lochmaben, 1614/1616. [CLC#1702/1757]

MURRAY, JOHN, in Banks of Hillis, parish of Lochrutton, 1620. [NAS.CS7/335]

MURRAY, JOHN, the Earl of Annandale, was granted the manor of Ballyweele and Castle Murray in Ireland, by King Charles I in 1639. [CLC#3315]

MURRAY, JOHN, son of the late Richard Murray of Broughton, Wigtownshire, and his wife Anna, acquired Killibegs, County Donegal, in 1698. [CLC#2890]

NEILIE, SAMUEL, arrived in Dumfries during 1690 from Ireland. [NAS.CH2.537.15.1/30]

NEILL, JOHN, in Hemayins, parish of Caerlaverock, 1619. [NAS.CS7/335/109]

NEILSON, CUBBIE, in Lawstoun, parish of Lochrutton, 1620. [NAS.CS7/335]

NEILSON, ELIZABETH, a merchant in Moffat, 1699. [NAS.RD4.84.679]

NEILSON, GEORGE, a merchant in Lockerbie, 1699. [NAS.RD2.82.1057]

NEILSON, GILBERT, in Merfass, parish of Urr, testament, 1593, Commissary of Edinburgh. [NAS]

NEILSON, GILBERT, in Merquhirn, parish of Kirkpatrick-Durham, 1614. [CLC#1702]

NEILSON, JOHN, of Corsock, 1613. [CLC#1690]

NEILSON, ROBERT, in Drummukloch, parish of Inch, spouse Christian McKennar, testament, 1591, Commissary of Edinburgh. [NAS]

NEILSON, ROBERT, a merchant in Dumfries, 1622. [NAS.E71.10.5]

NEILSON, WILLIAM, dean of Dumfries, 1697. [NAS.RD2.80/1.603]

NEVIN, JOHN, in Blackbrigs, parish of Balmaghie, 1619. [NAS.CS7/335/63]

NEWALL, ADAM, of Barskioch, born 1638, died 6 February 1712, his wife (1) Sarah, born 1640, died 1670, (2) Elizabeth, born 1657, died 27 January 1723. [Dalry gravestone]

NEWALL, JOHN, of Barskioch, born 1592, died 1658, his wife Marion, born 1601, died 1671. [Dalry gravestone]

NEWALL, JOHN, a messenger in Dumfries, deed, 1699. [NAS.RD2.83.562]

NEWALL, THOMAS, heir to his father Archibald Newall a burgess of Dumfries, re lands in parish of Dumfries. [NAS.Retours, Dumfries#11]

NEWALL, WILLIAM, a merchant in Dumfries, 1621. [NAS.E71.10.5]

NICOLSON, ARCHIBALD, in Rigside, testament, 1682, Commissary of Dumfries, 1686. [NAS]

NICOLSON, ROBERT, a cordiner in the parish of Caerlaverock, 1619. [NAS.CS7/335/109]

NOBLE, THOMAS, servant in Carruthers, testament, 1638, Commissary of Dumfries, 1686. [NAS]

NOBLE, WALTER, master of the Mayflower of Whithorn, 1681. [NAS.E72.19.1]

OSBURNE, JAMES, in Keir, testament, 1657, Commissary of Dumfries, 1686. [NAS]

OUSTEAN, WILLIAM, in Lanrigsland, parish of Caerlaverock, 1619. [NAS.CS7/335/109]

PADZEAN, JANET, in Glen, testament, 1674, Commissary of Dumfries, 1686. [NAS]

PAIN, JOHN, in Burnside of Mabie, testament, 1627, Commissary of Dumfries, 1686. [NAS]

PAISLEY, JOHN, in Erkinholm, testament, 1681, Commissary of Dumfries, 1686. [NAS]

PALMER, JOHN, a merchant in Dumfries, 1622. [NAS.E71.10.5]

PARK, ANDREW, in Nether Cassa, testament, 1674, Commissary of Dumfries, 1686. [NAS]

PATTERSON, EDWARD, in Blackshaw, parish of Caerlaverock, 1619. [NAS.CS7/335/109]

PATERSON, EDWARD, at Greenmill and at Bankend, parish of Caerlaverock, 1619. [NAS.CS7/335/109]

PATERSON, JAMES, in Greenhill, parish of Moffat, 1620. [NAS.CS7/335/265]

PATERSON, JOHN, in Glencaple, parish of Caerlaverock, 1619. [NAS.CS7/335/109]

PATERSON, JOHN, schoolmaster of Moffat, father of William an apprentice in Edinburgh, 1657. [Edinburgh Register of Apprentices]

PATERSON, PATRICK, provost of Stranraer, 1699. [NAS.RD3.91.732]

PATERSON, ROBERT, a merchant in Dumfries, 1622. [NAS.E71.10.5]

PATERSON, SUSANNA, arrived in Dumfries during 1690 from Ireland. [NAS.CH2.537.15.1/30]

PATERSON, THOMAS, arrived in Dumfries during 1690 from Ireland. [NAS.CH2.537.15.1/28, 96]

PATTERSON, WILLIAM, in the parish of Moffat, 1620. [NAS.CS7/335/265]

PATISON, CUTHBERT, a merchant in Dumfries, 1621. [NAS.E71.10.5]

PAXTON, WILLIAM, a merchant in Lockerbie, testament, 1658, Commissary of Dumfries, 1686. [NAS]

PHILIPSON, JOHN, master of the Three Brothers of Dumfries, trading with Bordeaux, 1682. [NAS.E72.6.7]

PICKERSGILL, WILLIAM, a merchant, spouse Margaret Blythe, testament, 1681, Commissary of Dumfries. [NAS]

PORTEOUS, ADAM, in Huttonhill, parish of Dryfesdale, 1620. [NAS.CS7/335/294]

PORTEOUS, JOHN, in Windays, parish of Dryfesdale, 1620. [NAS.CS7/335/294]

PORTEOUS, JOHN, in Dryisholme, parish of Dryfesdale, 1620. [NAS.CS7/335/294]

PORTEOUS, JOHN, in Peelhouse, parish of Dryfesdale, 1620. [NAS.CS7/335/294]

PORTEOUS, THOMAS, of Fruid, parish of Moffat, 1620. [NAS.CS7/335/265]

PORTEOUS, WILLIAM, in Greenknow, parish of Dryfesdale, 1620. [NAS.CS7/335/294]

PORTER, JAMES, miller at Cairn Mill, testament, 1674, Commissary of Dumfries, 1686. [NAS]

PORTER, JOHN, in Stranehannay, parish of Dalry, testament, 1595, Commissary of Edinburgh. [NAS]

POTT, THOMAS, in Fuldoris, parish of Dryfesdale, 1620. [NAS.CS7/335/294]

POTT, WILLIAM, in Huttonhill, parish of Dryfesdale, 1620. [NAS.CS7/335/294]

PRINGALL, ROBERT, Customs officer at Dumfries, 1613-1615. [NAS.E74.1.4; E74.2.4]

PRITCHARD, DAVID, master of the Margaret of Dumfries, 1689. [NAS.E72.6.13]

PURSE, WALTER, in Dumfries, testament, 1680, Commissary of Dumfries, 1686. [NAS]

RAE, DAVID, in Uliack, parish of Balmaghie, 1619. [NAS.CS7/335/63]

RAE, DAVID, in Edgartoun, parish of Balmaghie, 1619. [NAS.CS7/335/63]

RAE, JANET, in the Woodend in the Bankend, parish of Caerlaverock, 1619. [NAS.CS7/335/109]

RAE, JOHN, in Are, parish of Balmaghie, 1619. [NAS.CS7/335/63]

RAE, JOHN, a merchant in Dumfries, 1621. [NAS.E71.10.5]

RAINING, JAMES, a merchant in Dumfries, testament, 1686, Commissary of Dumfries, 1686. [NAS]

RAMMEIS, JOHN, a burgess of Dumfries, testament, 1600, Commissary of Edinburgh. [NAS]

RANALD, KATHERINE, in Glencaple, parish of Caerlaverock, 1619. [NAS.CS7/335/109]

RANING, HERBERT, a burgess of Dumfries, spouse Malie Kirkpatrick, testament, 1600, Commissary of Edinburgh. [NAS]

RASPER, JOHN, in Killilung, testament, 1678, Commissary of Dumfries, 1686. [NAS]

RAWLING, EDWARD, in the parish of Caerlaverock, 1619. [NAS.CS7/335/109]

RAWLING, JOHN, in Glencaple, parish of Caerlaverock, 1619. [NAS.CS7/335/109]

RAWLING, MARK, in Glencaple, parish of Caerlaverock, 1619. [NAS.CS7/335/109]

RAWLING, SAMUEL, in Glenhowen, parish of Caerlaverock, 1619. [NAS.CS7/335/109]

REDDICK, JOHN, of Dalbeattie, a debtor, 'put to the horn' in 1620. [RPCS.XII.204]

REDFORD, ANDREW, in Hewcleuch, parish of Moffat, 1620. [NAS.CS7/335/265]

REDPATH, WILLIAM, a merchant in Dumfries, 1621. [NAS.E71.10.5]

REID, ALEXANDER, in Losset, parish of Kirkcolm, testament, 1599, Commissary of Edinburgh. [NAS]

REID, HENRY, in Ragaquhat, parish of Dryfesdale, 1620. [NAS.CS7/335/294]; spouse Janet Boyd, testament, 1657, Commissary of Dumfries. [NAS]

REID, JAMES, in the parish of Moffat, 1620. [NAS.CS7/335/265]

REID, THOMAS, in Greenhill, parish of Moffat, 1620. [NAS.CS7/335/265]

REID, WILLIAM, in Broomholm, parish of Moffat, 1620. [NAS.CS7/335/265]

RENNICK, ROBERT, in Newbigging, testament, 1687, Commissary of Dumfries, 1686. [NAS]

RERICK, ROBERT, in Barnehourie, Cowen, testament, 1608, Commissary of Edinburgh. [NAS]

RICHARDSON, JANET, born 1641, widow of William Galloway in Lipnoch and wife of Reverend John Reid minister of Carsphain, died 31 December 1730. [Carsphairn gravestone]

RICHARDSON, JOHN, a merchant in Dumfries, 1622. [NAS.E71.10.5]

RICHARDSON, JOHN, a resident of Lochmaben, 1642. [LCC#45]

RICHARDSON, JOHN, from Borgue, Kirkcudbrightshire, a Covenanter who was transported to Barbados in 1679, shipwrecked. [RBM]

RIDDICK, ARCHIBALD, in Busse, testament, 1673, Commissary of Dumfries, 1686. [NAS]

RIGG, GEORGE, a merchant in Dumfries, 1622. [NAS.E71.10.5]

RIGG, WILLIAM, in Lawstoun, parish of Lochrutton, 1620. [NAS.CS7/335]

RITCHIE, JOHN, in Moffat, testament, 1690, Commissary of Dumfries, 1686. [NAS]

ROBERTSON, JOHN, a vagabond and robber in Annandale, to be caught and transported to the American Plantations, 1671. [RPCS.III.428]

ROBERTSON, JOHN, master of the Hopewell of Kirkcudbright, 1673. [NAS.E72.6.2]

ROBISON, JOHN, in Cormehead, parish of Lochrutton, 1620. [NAS.CS7/335]

ROBISON, JOHN, master of the Good Fortune of Kirkcudbright, 1681. [NAS.E72.6.5]

ROBSON, ADAM, in Schaw, parish of Parton, testament, 1594, Commissary of Edinburgh. [NAS]

ROBSON, ADAM, the younger, in Schaw, parish of Parton, testament, 1598, Commissary of Edinburgh. [NAS]

ROBSON, CHRISTOPHER, a merchant councillor of Lochmaben, 1684. [LCC#179]

ROBSON, CHRISTOPHER, a tailor and councillor of Lochmaben, 1684. [LCC#179]

ROBSON, JAMES, in Overdeadside, parish of Lochrutton, 1620. [NAS.CS7/335/311]

ROBSON, JOHN, in Waterhead, parish of Lochrutton, 1620. [NAS.CS7/335]

ROBSON, JOHN, in Barcloy, spouse Jean Blair, testament, 1657, Commissary of Dumfries. [NAS]

ROBSON, JOHN, a wright and councillor of Lochmaben, 1684. [LCC#179]

ROBSON, ROBERT, in Netherbarfell, parish of Lochrutton, 1620. [NAS.CS7/335/311]

ROBSON, ROBERT, in Dinkow, spouse Bessie Aitken, testament, 1659, Commissary of Dumfries. [NAS]

ROBSON, THOMAS, in Muncraig, his wife Janet Robson, testament, 1606, Commissary of Edinburgh. [NAS]

ROBSON, WALTER, in Barlay, parish of Lochrutton, 1620. [NAS.CS7/335]

ROBSON, WILLIAM, in Collochane, parish of Terregles, testament, 1600, Commissary of Edinburgh. [NAS]

ROBSON, WILLIAM, a resident of Lochmaben, 1642. [LCC#45]

RODDAN, HOMER, possibly from Kirkmaho, Dumfries-shire, emigrated via Liverpool to Virginia in 1698. [Liverpool Record Office, HQ325.2FRE][RPCS.VIII.640]

RODDAN, JOHN, in Dinkow, testament, 1657, Commissary of Dumfries. [NAS]

RODDICK, HEW, a miller, testament, 1658, Commissary of Dumfries, 1686. [NAS]

RODGER, WILLIAM, master of the Margaret of Dumfries, 1690. [NAS.E72.6.18]

ROGERSON, JOHN, and spouse Janet Corsbie in Closeburn Mill, testament, 1674, Commissary of Dumfries, 1686. [NAS]

ROME, JOHN, a merchant in Dumfries, 1621, trading with Flanders, 1622. [NAS.E71.10.5]

ROPER, WILLIAM, in Hall of Barquhar, parish of Lochrutton, 1620. [NAS.CS7/335]

RORISON, ANDREW, in Auchenstroan, testament, 1674, Commissary of Dumfries, 1686. [NAS]

ROSPER, THOMAS, from Glencairn, Nithsdale, a Covenanter who was transported to Barbados in 1679, shipwrecked. [RBM]

RULE, JOHN, in Quaarelwood, parish of Kirkmahoe, testament, 1640, Commissary of Dumfries, 1686. [NAS]

RULE, ROBERT, a notary burgess of Dumfries, testament, 1657, Commissary of Dumfries, 1686. [NAS]

RUSSELL, JOHN, a resident of Lochmaben, 1642. [LCC#45]

RUSSELL, SIMON, a resident of Lochmaben, 1642. [LCC#45]

RUTHERFORD, SAMUEL, born in Nisbet, Roxburghshire, in 1600, minister of Anwoth, died there 1661. [Anwoth gravestone]

SANDART, ROBERT, in Muirhouse, testament, 1687, Commissary of Dumfries, 1686. [NAS]

SANDERSON, JOHN, in Corbellie, testament, 1626, Commissary of Dumfries, 1686. [NAS]

SAVAGE, JAMES, in Sanquhar, testament, 1641, Commissary of Dumfries, 1686. [NAS]

SCHAW, JOHN, a merchant in Dumfries, 1621. [NAS.E71.10.5]

SCOTT, ADAM, a merchant in Dumfries, 1622. [NAS.E71.10.5]

SCOTT, ANDREW, in Newhall of Garnesalloch, testament, 1597, Commissary of Edinburgh. [NAS]

SCOTT, JOHN, in Meikleholmside, parish of Moffat, 1620. [NAS.CS7/335/265]

SCOTT, JOHN, arrived in Dumfries during 1690 from Ireland. [NAS.CH2.537.15.1/127]

SCOTT, ROBERT, master of the Mariann of Dumfries, 1689. [NAS.E72.6.20/21]

SCOTT, ROBERT, born 1669, resident of Red Knox, died 2 January 1739, his wife Marion Carson, born 1670, died 3 November 1738. [Buittle gravestone]

SCOTT, WALTER, a merchant in Dumfries, 1621. [NAS.E71.10.5]

SHANKLAND, ROBERT, in Bogrie, parish of Lochrutton, 1620. [NAS.CS7.335.311]

SHARP, JOHN, heir to his father John Sharp a merchant bailie of Dumfries, 1656. [NAS.Retours, Dumfries#229]

SHARP, ROBERT, in Barjarg, spouse Agnes Braithnoch, testament, 1677, Commissary of Dumfries. [NAS]

SHARP, THOMAS, a merchant burgess of Dumfries, spouse Margaret Beck, testament, 1627, Commissary of Dumfries. [NAS]

SHAW, JOHN, in Thirdpart, parish of Lochrutton, 1620. [NAS.CS7.335.311]

SHAW, MARGARET, in Broomhouse, parish of Dryfesdale, 1620. [NAS.CS7/335/294]

SHILESTON, THOMAS, from Hillend, Dunspurn, a Covenater in Dumfries Tolbooth, transported to East New Jersey in 1685. [RPCS.XI.155/291]

SHILTHOMAS, W., in Kirkcudbright, 1641. [NAS.E73.9.7]

SHITLINGTON, JOHN, in Crawfordston, testament, 1677, Commissary of Dumfries, 1686. [NAS]

SHORT, GEORGE, a Covenanter killed in the parish of Tongland, 1685. [Balmaghie gravestone]

SHORT, ROBERT, in Bargatoun, parish of Balmaghie, 1619. [NAS.CS7/335/63]

SHORT, ROBERT, in Bleinmack, parish of Balmaghie, 1619. [NAS.CS7/335/63]

SHORT, WILLIAM, in Barledzow, parish of Sorbie, spouse Katherine Maxwell, testament, 1592, Commissary of Edinburgh. [NAS]

SHORTRIG, JOHN, of Marieholm, testament, 1600, Commissary of Edinburgh. [NAS]

SIMONTON, JAMES, in Skailinaillis, testament, 1657, Commissary of Dumfries, 1686. [NAS]

SIMSON, WILLIAM, a litster burgess of Dumfries, testament, 1594, Commissary of Edinburgh. [NAS]

SINCLAIR, ELIZABETH, in Carsemannoch, parish of Minnigaff, testament, 1592, Commissary of Edinburgh. [NAS]

SINCLAIR, JOHN, in Ardoch, parish of Dalry, testament, 1598, Commissary of Edinburgh. [NAS]

SINCLAIR, JOHN, in Brekoch, parish of Balmaghie, 1619. [NAS.CS7/335/63]

SINCLAIR, WILLIAM, in Carswada, parish of Lochrutton, 1620. [NAS.CS7/335/311]

SLEWMAN, JOHN, a burgess of Wigtown, testament, 1599, Commissary of Edinburgh. [NAS]

SMITH, EDWARD, master of the Hopewell of Whithorn, 1690. [NAS.E72.6.21]

SMITH, JOHN, a resident of Lochmaben, 1642. [LCC#45]

SMITH, JOHN, from Glencairn, Nithsdale, a Covenanter who was transported to Barbados in 1679, shipwrecked. [RBM]

SMITH, JOHN, from Dalry, Galloway, a Covenanter who was transported to Barbados in 1679, shipwrecked. [RBM]

SMITH, ROBERT, a resident of Lochmaben, 1642. [LCC#45]

SMYTH, JOHN, in Uliock, parish of Balmaghie, 1619. [NAS.CS7/335/63]

SMYTH, NICOLL, in Hillhead, parish of Dryfesdale, 1620. [NAS.CS7/335/294]

SMYTH, PATRICK, in Lochenbrock, parish of Balmaghie, 1619. [NAS.CS7/335/63]

SMYTH, ROBERT, the elder, a councillor of Lochmaben, 1684. [LCC#179]

SMYTH, WILLIAM, in Tilbertmoir, testament, 1592, Commissary of Edinburgh. [NAS]

SMYTH, WILLIAM, in Peelhouse, parish of Dryfesdale, 1620. [NAS.CS7/335/294]

SMYTH, WILLIAM, in Lockerbie, parish of Dryfesdale, 1620. [NAS.CS7/335/294]

SNEDDON, JOHN, in Wormanbie, spouse Jean Broadfoot, testament, 1659, Commissary of Dumfries. [NAS]

SOMERVILLE, JOHN, a writer in Dumfries, 1697. [NAS.RD2.81/1.438]

SPALSIE, JOHN, a surgeon from Kirkcudbright, died at Darien, 1699, testament, 1707, Commissary of Edinburgh. [NAS]

SPENS, JOHN, a merchant burgess of Dumfries, 1621; testament, 1638, Commissary of Dumfries, 1686.[NAS.E71.10.5]

SPRATT, JOHN, a merchant from Wigtown, Galloway, a member of the Scots Charitable Society of Boston in 1685. [NEHGS/SCS]

SPROAT, KATHERINE, daughter of John Sproat a burgess of Kirkcudbright, and William Sproat, son of the late William Sproat in Donnachadee, Ireland, marriage contract, 1666. [Kirkcudbright Sheriff Court Deeds #54]

SPROTT, ANDREW, from Borgue, Kirkcudbrightshire, a Covenanter who was transported to Barbados in 1679, shipwrecked. [RBM]

SPROTT, JOHN, in Laich Borgue, parish of Borgue, testament, 1600, Commissary of Edinburgh. [NAS]

SPROTT, WILLIAM, from Clontarch, a Covenanter transported to East New Jersey in 1685. [RPCS.X.154/612]

STAFFAN, JOHN, master of the John of Kirkcudbright, 1673. [NAS.E72.6.2]

STARMOUNT, JOHN, and spouse Sibella Murray in Aiket, testament, 1658, Commissary of Dumfries, 1686. [NAS]

STEILL, ALEXANDER, in Langholm, parish of Dryfesdale, 1620. [NAS.CS7/335/294]

STEILL, ALLAN, in Peelhouse, parish of Dryfesdale, 1620. [NAS.CS7/294]

STEILL, ARCHIE, the younger, in Greenknow, parish of Dryfesdale, 1620. [NAS.CS7/335/294]

STEILL, GAVIN, a merchant in Dumfries, 1622. [NAS.E71.10.5]

STEILL, GEORGE, the elder, in Peelhouse, parish of Dryfesdale, 1620. [NAS.CS7/335/294]

STEILL, JAMES, in Huttonhill, parish of Dryfesdale, 1620. [NAS.CS7/335/294]

STEILL, JOHN, a merchant burgess of Kirkcudbright, testament, 1593, Commissary of Edinburgh. [NAS]

STEILL, JOHN, in Auchinslark, parish of Dryfesdale, 1620. [NAS.CS7/335/294]

STEILL, RICHIE, in Skar, parish of Dryfesdale, 1620. [NAS.CS7/335/294]

STEILL, SIMON, a merchant in Dumfries, 1622. [NAS.E71.10.5]

STEILL, WILLIAM, in Peelhouse, parish of Dryfesdale, 1620. [NAS.CS7/335/294]

STEILL, WILLIAM, in Torwood, parish of Dryfesdale, 1620. [NAS.CS7/335/294]

STEWART, ALEXANDER, of Garleis, heir to his father Alexander Stewart of Garleis, 1600, Wigtown. [NAS.S/H]

STEWART, JAMES, a merchant burgess of Dumfries, testament, 1591, Commissary of Edinburgh. [NAS]

STEWART, JOHN, in Crofthere, parish of Kirkconnell, spouse Helen Gordon, testament, 1590, Commissary of Edinburgh. [NAS]

STEWART, JOHN, in Glenluchock, fled to Ireland in 1684. [Penningham KSR, 19.2.1711]

STEWART, PATRICK, in Caldoneis, parish of Minnigaff, spouse Margaret McKie, testament, 1593, Commissary of Edinburgh. [NAS]

STEWART, PATRICK, a burgess of Wigtown, testament, 1598, Commissary of Edinburgh. [NAS]

STEWART, ROBERT, of Ardoch, died in February 1678, his wife Barbara Stuart, died 1697. [Dalry gravestone]

STEWART, ROBERT, son of Major Robert Stewart of Ardoch, killed as a Covenanter, 1684. [Dalry gravestone]

STEWART, THOMAS, born in Galloway during 1666, a merchant in Bridgetown, Barbados, died in Chelsea, England, 1722, probate, 1723, Barbados.

STEWART, WILLIAM, of Fintallich, parish of Penninghame, testament, 1598, Commissary of Edinburgh. [NAS]

STEWART, WILLIAM, in Bargennan, testament, 1599, Commissary of Edinburgh. [NAS]

STEWART, WILLIAM, born in Whithorn, Wigtownshire, son of Archibald Stewart, settled in County Tyrone by 1643. [MA#75]

STITT, AGNES, in Lochrutton Gait, parish of Lochrutton, 1620. [NAS.CS7/335]

STOBRIG, JOHN, the elder, in Stobrig, parish of Caerlaverock, 1619. [NAS.CS7/335/109]

STOBRIG, JOHN, the younger, in Stobrig, parish of Caerlaverock, 1619. [NAS.CS7/335/109]

STOTT, JOHN, in Hemayns, parish of Caerlaverock, 1619. [NAS.CS7/335/109]

STROWAN, WALTER, in Rynganey, testament, 1594, Commissary of Edinburgh. [NAS]

STRUDGEON, ANDREW, of Corrie, parish of Balmaghie, 1619. [NAS.CS7/335/63]

STURGEON, EDWARD, in Wraithis, a witness, 1611; testament, 1625, Commissary of Dumfries, 1686. [NAS] [CLC#1620]

STURGEON, JOHN, in Carmuck, parish of Caerlaverock, 1619. [NAS.CS7/335/109]

TAGGART, JOHN, from Roaderheuk, Annandale, a Covenanter who was transported to East New Jersey in 1685. [RPCS.XI.155]

TAGGART, WILLIAM, in Unerwood, testament, 1684, Commissary of Dumfries, 1686. [NAS]

TAILFOUR, JAMES, in Kirkdeoch, testament, 1598, Commissary of Edinburgh. [NAS]

TAIT, JOHN, a clerk in Closeburn, testament, 1657, Commissary of Dumfries, 1686. [NAS]

TAIT, MATTHEW, a merchant burgess of Dumfries, testament, 1597, Commissary of Edinburgh. [NAS]

TAYLOR, JOHN, the elder and the younger, in Mantuarig, parish of Dryfesdale, 1620. [NAS.CS7/335/294]

TAYLOR, JOHN, Deacon of the Wrights in Dumfries, testament, 1649, Commissary of Dumfries, 1686. [NAS]

TELFER, THOMAS, in Glencouband, spouse Bessie Airnes, testament, 1657, Commissary of Dumfries. [NAS]

THOMSON, ADAM, a merchant in Dumfries, 1621. [NAS.E71.10.5]

THOMSON, ARCHIBALD, a merchant in Dumfries, 1621. [NAS.E71.10.5]

THOMSON, ARCHIBALD, spouse Blanche Beattie, testament, 1656, Commissary of Dumfries. [NAS]

THOMSON, DAVID, in Deanstoun, parish of Lochrutton, 1620. [NAS.CS7.335.311]

THOMSON, JOHN, in Hills, parish of Lochrutton, 1620. [NAS.CS7/335]

THOMSON, JOHN, schoolmaster of Dumfries, husband of Agnes Douglas, 1661. [NAS.RD3.1.501]

THOMSON, PETER, his wife Elizabeth Gibson, parents of William, died May 1694. [Colvend gravestone]

THOMSON, WILLIAM, from Borgue, Kirkcudbrightshire, a Covenanter who was transported to Barbados in 1679, shipwrecked. [RBM]

THOMSON, WILLIAM, died 27 March 1657, his wife Janet McLellan (?), died 1684. [Colvend gravestone]

THOMSON, WILLIAM, in Kirkgunzeon, who was accused of adultery, fled to Ireland in 1691. [NAS.CH2.537.15.2/85-197]

THORNEBRAND, MATTHEW, a merchant burgess of Dumfries, testament, 1679, Commissary of Dumfries, 1686. [NAS]

TOD, AGNES, in Kirkcroft, parish of Lochrutton, 1620. [NAS.CS7/335]

TOD, JOHN, born 1719, a surgeon apothecary, died in February 1700. [Buittle gravestone]

TOD, QUENTIN, a goat-thief in Kirkcudbright, transported to Barbados in 1666. [RPCS.II.134]

TOSHACH, ALEXANDER, schoolmaster of Moffat, father of James an apprentice bookbinder, 1699. [NAS.RD4.46.928]

TROTTER, ELIZABETH, arrived in Dumfries from Ireland in 1690. [NAS.CH2.537.15.1/30, 61]

TURNER, WILLIAM, in Carse of Arbigland, testament, 1685, Commissary of Dumfries, 1686. [NAS]

TWYNHOLM, JOHN, in Speddoch, testament, 1658, Commissary of Dumfries, 1686. [NAS]

UMPHRAY, WILLIAM, in Tounghouse, testament, 1641, Commissary of Dumfries, 1686. [NAS]

UNDERWOOD, RICHARD, a merchant in Dumfries, 1621. [NAS.E71.10.5]

VANS, JOHN, of Longcaster, heir to his father Patrick Vans of Barnebarroch, Wigtown, 1600. [NAS.S/H]

VERNER, THOMAS, born 1632, minister of Balmaclellan, died 10 September 1716. [Balmaclellan gravestone]

WALKER, ADAM, a burgess of Dumfries, spouse Janet Crawford, testament, 1591, Commissary of Edinburgh. [NAS]

WALKER, EDWARD, in Nether Gribton, spouse Agnes Aitken, testament, 1684, Commissary of Dumfries. [NAS]

WALKER, GAVIN, in Dalton, spouse Janet Archibaldson, testament, 1626, Commissary of Dumfries. [NAS]

WALKER, WILLIAM, in Moffatstown, spouse Janet Carmichael, testament, 1624, Commissary of Dumfries. [NAS]

WALLACE, JAMES, a burgess of Dumfries, testament, 1596, Commissary of Edinburgh. [NAS]

WALLACE, JAMES, in Five shilling land, parish of Balmaghie, 1619. [NAS.CS7/335/63]

WALLACE, JOHN, in Glencaple, parish of Caerlaverock, 1619. [NAS.CS7/335/109]

WALLACE, ROBERT, in Carzeill, testament, 1595, Commissary of Edinburgh. [NAS]

WALLACE, THOMAS, in Drumbank, parish of Kirkmahoe, testament, 1599, Commissary of Edinburgh. [NAS]

WALLET, ANDREW, in Glen Head Croft, parish of Kirkpatrick-Irongray, testament, 1642, Commissary of Dumfries, 1686. [NAS]

WALLET, ANDREW, from Irongray, Dumfries-shire, a Covenanter who was transported to Barbados in 1679, shipwrecked. [RBM]

WARDEN, LOUIS, a servant, 1616. [CLC#1758]

WATSON, JAMES, in Nunsholme, testament, 1679, Commissary of Dumfries, 1686. [NAS]

WATSON, JANET, in Dumfries, testament, 1658, Commissary of Dumfries, 1686. [NAS]

WAUCH, ISABEL, in Meikleholmside, parish of Moffat, 1620. [NAS.CS7/335/265]

WAUGH, DAVID, in Barnhill, parish of Kirkpatrick, testament, 1593, Commissary of Edinburgh. [NAS]

WAUGH, ROBERT, in Ingeston, testament, 1687, Commissary of Dumfries, 1686. [NAS]

WEIR, JOHN, absconded from Dumfries to Ireland in 1692. [NAS.CH2.537.15.2/145-146]

WEIR, WILLIAM, a merchant in Dumfries, 1622. [NAS.E71.10.5]

WELLIS, GEORGE, a chapman in Dumfries, testament, 1682, Commissary of Dumfries, 1686. [NAS]

WELSH, EDWARD, in Nethercroft, parish of Lochrutton, 1620. [NAS.CS7/335]

WELSH, ROBERT, in Half Mark, testament, 1607, Commissary of Edinburgh. [NAS]

WHARRIE, CLEMENT, in Locherwoods, testament, 1690, Commissary of Dumfries, 1686. [NAS]

WHINKERSTANES, JOHN, a merchant in Crossmichael, testament, 1604, Commissary of Edinburgh. [NAS]

WHITE, JOHN, in Crokroy, testament, 1626, Commissary of Dumfries, 1686. [NAS]

WHITEFORD, ADAM, in Tochridge, 1636, 1654. [RGS.X.588]

WHITEHEAD, ANDREW, in Little Merkland, parish of Lochrutton, 1620. [NAS.CS7.335.311]

WHITEHEAD, HERBERT, in Barncleugh, parish of Kirkpatrick-Irongray, testament, 1600, Commissary of Edinburgh. [NAS]

WHYTE, ALAN, at St John's Chapel, parish of Saulseat, testament, 1600, Commissary of Edinburgh. [NAS]

WIGHOLME, JOHN, a burgess of Sanquhar, testament, 1659, Commissary of Dumfries, 1686. [NAS]

WIGHTMAN, JOHN, in Ruiken, testament, 1657, Commissary of Dumfries, 1686. [NAS]

WILKIE, ADAM, in Coats, testament, 1678, Commissary of Dumfries, 1686. [NAS]

WILKIN, JOHN, in Corswada, parish of Lochrutton, 1620. [NAS.CS7/335]

WILLIAMSON, JOHN, a merchant in Dumfries, trading with Flanders, 1622. [NAS.E71.10.5]

WILLIAMSON, WILLIAM, a merchant in Dumfries, 1622. [NAS.E71.10.5]

WILSON, ANDREW, in Garglen, testament, 1596, Commissary of Edinburgh. [NAS]

WILSON, ANDREW, in Tynron, spouse Euphan Bromerig, testament, 1600, Commissary of Edinburgh. [NAS]

WILSON, ANDREW, a merchant in Dumfries, 1621, 1622. [NAS.E71.10.5]

WILSON, JOHN, in Head, parish of Lochrutton, 1620. [NAS.CS7.335.311]

WILSON, JOHN, in Greenhill, parish of Moffat, 1620. [NAS.CS7/335/265]

WILSON, JOHN, a merchant in Dumfries, 1622. [NAS.E71.10.5]

WILSON, LEONARD, in Erectstone, parish of Moffat, 1620. [NAS.CS7/335/265]

WILSON, PATRICK, in Edgarton, parish of Balmaghie, 1619. [NAS.CS7/335/63]

WILSON, WILLIAM, from Galloway, a Covenanter transported to East New Jersey in 1685. [RPCS.XI.154]

WOLL, JOHN, in Amisfieldton, testament, 1625, Commissary of Dumfries, 1686. [NAS]

WOOD, DAVID, in Ruthwell, testament, 1674, Commissary of Dumfries, 1686. [NAS]

WOOD, JOHN, in Corswada, parish of Lochrutton, 1620. [NAS.CS7/335]

WRIGHT, JAMES, in Datonhook, parish of Dryfesdale, 1620. [NAS.CS7/335/294]

WRIGHT, ROBERT, a carrier burgess in Dumfries, spouse Margaret Adamson, testament, 1681, Commissary of Dumfries. [NAS]

WRIGHT, SAMUEL, master of the Robert of Dumfries, 1690. [NAS.E72.6.18]

WRIGHT, THOMAS, a merchant burgess of Dumfries, spouse Marion Beck, testament, 1638, Commissary of Dumfries. [NAS]

WYLLIE, JAMES, a merchant in Dumfries, 1622. [NAS.E71.10.5]

YOUNG, ANDREW, a burgess of Kirkcudbright, testament, 1596, Commissary of Edinburgh. [NAS]

YOUNG, ANDREW, the youger, son of Andrew Young, a burgess of Kirkcudbright, testament, 1599, Commissary of Edinburgh. [NAS]

YOUNG, PATRICK, a surgeon in Dumfries, 1621. [RPCS.XII.586]

YOUNG, PATRICK, of Auchenskeoch, spouse Anna Buchanan, testament, 1657, Commissary of Dumfries. [NAS]

YOUNG, ROBERT, a vagabond and robber in Annandale, to be caught and transported to the American Plantations, 1671. [RPCS.III.428]

CPSIA information can be obtained
at www.ICGtesting.com
Printed in the USA
FFOW01n0507100317
33241FF